GYM RATS

By Wendell Trogdon

*To Mike,
With best wishes!
Wendell Trogdon
1994*

HIGHLANDE**R** PRESS

Dedication

To the men and women who coach, the sons and daughters who play for them, and the spouses and mothers who share their glories and disappointments.

Highlander Press First Edition
Copyright 1990 by Wendell Trogdon
All rights reserved under International and Pan-American
Copyright Conventions. Published in the United States by
The Highlander Press, Evanston, Illinois.
Local distribution by Wendell Trogdon,
Mooresville, Indiana
ISBN 0-913617-12-1

Cover art by Gary Varvel
Cover and book design by Martin Northway
Typography by Ampersand Associates, Inc., Chicago

A list of Highlander Press titles is available by sending an SASE to:
The Highlander Press, 1108 Davis #104 Evanston, IL 60201

Table of Contents

Introduction

Being a father is the most difficult thing a man can ever do. If he doesn't do it right, he can't do it over.   —*Anonymous*

* * *

Most men work in obscurity at the complex task of being a father. Men who coach their sons do it in view of a thousand critics, their every move subject to review.

In Indiana, men who coach their sons may be vilified in one game, glorified the next. Their sons, the gym rats of basketball, may be taunted as freshmen, booed as sophomores, lauded as juniors, and acclaimed as seniors.

This book is about some of the men who chose to coach their sons, and about the sons who performed for them.

Before we began our interviews, we thought this would be a book limited to basketball. That changed after conversations with coaches and their sons.

Their stories, of course, *are* about basketball. But they also are about life, about joy and heartache, about family life, about dedication, about mental toughness, and about survival under duress.

And there are stories about the love of fathers for their sons, about the devotion of sons to their fathers and about mothers who kept that love and devotion from splintering in moments of disharmony.

"GYM RATS"

"Gym rat" isn't in any dictionary we can find, but basketball fans know what it means. A "gym rat" is a youngster who spends much, if not all, his free time in the gymnasium, usually with a basketball in his hands and a goal in his sights.

He often is the son of a basketball coach. He is in the gym because that's where his dad often is. And all sons, at least at an early age, want to be with their fathers.

"Gym rats" start hanging around the gym when they are two or three years old, or as soon as their parents will take them there.

Some hide behind the front seat of their dad's car, then pop up when he reaches the gym. As they grow older, they become team mascots, statisticians, ball boys, or keepers of the water bottles. They sit with the team, listen to what is said at time-outs, learn strategy, and adopt players as their idols.

"Gym rats" start playing basketball themselves as soon as they are old enough. Some are on teams as first graders.

Most have been told by their fathers that the only way to become good at the sport is to play it. And they do—morning, noon, and night.

By the fifth or sixth grade, it becomes obvious some of them will be better than other players. Their exposure to the game has given them that edge. And they will continue to become better, following directions and drills laid out by their fathers, going through a list of workouts he has prescribed.

Some may be ready for the varsity as freshmen and move up to play for their dad. Others may be ready, but their fathers will let them stay on the freshman or junior varsity for a year, maybe more. A few may need more time to develop.

The first few times they play, fans wonder whether they are good enough. Some observers say the only reason they are allowed to play is because they are the coaches' sons. Some fans will boo them.

In the end, most coaches' sons will succeed, because as "gym rats" they have learned the art of survival.

ACKNOWLEDGEMENTS

Ask a coach to talk basketball and he'll set aside some time for you no matter how busy he is.

We contacted 28 present and former coaches and 24 of them agreed to cooperate in our research for this book. Each of the coaches was interviewed, mostly in the gymnasiums where they coach.

We visited with many of their sons, some of the coaches' wives, and talked basketball for hundreds of hours.

The coaches, players, and wives were candid in their comments about their roles in families where sons are coached by their fathers. They shared the good and the bad, the joy and disappointment, the upside and downside of father-son relationships in basketball.

This is not a complete report on all coaches who are or have been their sons' basketball mentors. Time did not permit that. But it is a representative group, both of coaches and sons.

You will read comments from veteran coaches like Jack Butcher, whose Loogootee teams have won 582 games; Norm Held, who has 502 victories; Phil Buck, whose teams have won 480 times, and Sam Alford, who started the 1989-90 season with 337 victories.

You will find sons of coaches, boys who grew up playing for their fathers, who now are coaches themselves. They include Joe Buck, head coach at Lapel; Bernie Butcher, head coach at Washington after a stint at South Knox; Brad Tucker, new head coach at South Knox; David Null, an assistant at Seymour, and Scott Heady, an assistant at Carmel.

There are three former Indiana high school "Mr. Basketballs" who played for their fathers, Billy (1968) and Dave Shepherd (1970) and Steve Alford (1983). (Kyle Macy, another Mr. Basketball [1975] played for his father, Bob, at Peru. And Mr. Basketballs Dave Colescott [1976] of Marion and Steve Collier [1974] of Southwestern at Hanover, also had fathers who were coaches.)

Other Indiana all-stars included here are Bill Butcher, Chad Tucker, Jeff Oliphant, and Jamie Matthews. (Craig Neal, who played for his father at Washington, also was an Indiana all-star in 1983. Matt Petty, whose father is coach at Wabash College, was a 1989 all-star from Crawfordsville.)

GYM RATS

Some Insights

LIKE FATHER, LIKE SON

"From the standpoint of the game of basketball, we [Dad and I] had almost telepathic communications. I could look at my dad. He wouldn't have to say anything, but I could tell what he wanted. It was almost a sixth sense, a communication I could convey to other players on the court.

"Coaches' kids are instilled with a lot of intangibles—leadership abilities, the ability to keep cool when things go crazy around you, the ability to think things through. Those are things you carry with you in later years.

"In banking there are times when I wonder how I was able to deal with certain situations. I ask myself, 'Where did that ability come from? Where did I get the composure to get this position and perform adequately, if not well?'

"Then I think back and I realize it may have come from Dad and from basketball.

"A coach is a teacher, who teaches men how to think, a gift you can't underestimate. Too many people have never been taught how to think. They don't know how to take on a situation and think it through."

—Bill Butcher, son of Coach Jack Butcher, Loogootee

MIXED EMOTIONS

"There are times, no doubt about it, that I'd rather that they [sons Chip and Richie] were playing for someone else. For their good, I think, they would be better off. Yet, it is something I wouldn't want to give up. It's a one-time thing and you are never going to have that chance again. But sometimes I wonder if it is best for them.

"They could be free like every other kid and not have to toe the line and obey every rule."

—Lafayette Coach Jim Hammel

A MATTER OF CHOICE

"We live at Bloomfield, but I enrolled my son Joey at Union-Dugger where I coached when he was in the seventh grade. I did that for two reasons. I thought he would be a decent basketball player and I wanted the opportunity to coach him. I had talked with Guy Glover, the athletic director at Bloomfield, who had coached his son. Mr. Glover told me it was an experience that I'd never forget. I haven't been disappointed."

—Joe Hart, who coaches his son, Joey

SECOND THOUGHTS

"I would have preferred, had it been possible at that time, to have sent my sons Joe and Larry to Anderson High School to play for Ray Estes. Knowing they might have beat me, I still think it would have been fairer to those two boys had they got to do that."

—Madison Heights Coach Phil Buck

* * *

Lives of "gym rats" have peaks and valleys. Here are some of many you will read about in this book:

STEVE ALFORD: Steve Alford was a freshman at New Castle when he tried to get his father's attention at basketball practice. "I yelled 'Dad.' He didn't come over. I yelled 'Dad' again. Finally he turned and walked, looking real stern and said, 'Look, when we're here I'm Coach. At home you can call me Dad.'

"That was the first time it really hit me that he was going to be the coach and not just 'Dad' all the time."

RYAN SORRELL: Ryan Sorrell was called for a charge with 20 seconds left in a holiday tournament game when his dad was coaching at Crawfordsville.

It was Ryan's fifth personal and Coach Mike Sorrell admits it was 50-50 whether it was a charge or a block: "But I had told Ryan several times not to come up the sidelines because it's an easier place to get called for a charge. We had a three-point lead, but I knew we were in real trouble, that without him we'd have a hard time bringing the ball up the floor. Sure enough, we lost the ball twice and got beat by a point.

"As Ryan came off the floor I got right in his ear and said, "You dumb ass. How many times do I have to tell you not to come up the side of the floor?'

"If that hadn't been my son, I would never had said that. What I did was wrong. I remember the look on his face as if it were yesterday."

RIC FORD: Ric Ford may still hold the record for the most pushups by a New Albany player. One night in practice he back-talked his dad, Jack. "Nobody talks back to the coach," Jack Ford says. "So I told him to do five.

He said something else and I ordered five more. The number kept going up until one of the other players said, 'Coach, lay off him.'"

LINC DARNER: During his junior year, Linc Darner had a great shooting spree when he averaged over 40 points per game for Anderson Highland. That didn't stop him from wanting to improve. On Saturday mornings after the games, he'd be in the driveway shooting, even shoveling off the snow once.

DAVID NULL: Coach Joe Null had his Edgewood team working on its press attack attack one night. His son, David, took the ball out of bounds, but the guards didn't move toward the ball. After about three seconds David yelled, "Time out," and said, "Come on, fellas. You have to move. I've got to get the ball in."

Coach Null said, "Let me do the coaching," and sent son David home.

David recalls, "I was upset about it. I took my shower and went home. I realized I hadn't shot my free throws, so I decided to go down to the park and shoot them.

"I didn't leave a note at the house, so Dad didn't know where I was when he came home. He finally found me down at the park. That's probably the lowest our relationship got," David Null recalls.

LARRY BUCK: Madison Heights had gone to the state finals in 1972. Larry Buck had been on that team as a junior. As a senior he was playing sixth man, but the Pirates were beaten in the final game of the sectional. "In fact," his dad, Coach Phil Buck, remembers, "we were embarrassed. We came home and nobody said anything about the game. I finally said, 'Well, we got waxed didn't we?'"

Larry, who had spent much of the time on the bench, replied, "Dad, I could have played better than that."

Phil Buck recalls: "I think I felt about as little right then as I have ever felt, because he was right."

The Home Team: Wives and Mothers

Coaches often are hired to be fired. When Phil Buck moved to Anderson he told Norma Jean, his wife:

"Don't spend any money on the house. We may not be here more than two years." After twenty-three years, she asked him if he thought it was safe to put some money into the place. "Better wait another year," he told her.

* * *

Wives and mothers play an important role in father-son, coach-player relationships. They are the glue that bonds fathers and sons. Here is what some coaches, sons, and mothers had to say:

COACH SAM ALFORD (New Castle): It was hard on me, it was hard on Steve, it was hard on Sean, but it was the hardest on Sharon.

It was possible when Sean was a sophomore that he would come home upset with reserve practice, Steve would come home upset with me, I'd come home upset with both of them and we'd all tell our stories to her and she was supposed to agree with all three of us. She was always caught in the middle. It was a tough situation for her.

COACH JIM MATTHEWS (New Washington): My wife, "Sugie," is an ideal person to support a basketball coach. She loves the game and she likes the competition and she has been supportive in every area. She will come to practice two or three times a week and bring ice cream. She has almost depleted our bank account at times [doing that]. I've been coaching for twenty-four years, and she has done it for twenty-four years.

CAROL ANDREW (wife of Coach Glenn Andrew, North Central, Sullivan County): You have to listen to comments, some good, some negative. That's the hardest part about being a coach's wife and the mother of players. Some of the comments are disturbing, especially the ones about my son. I know my husband can take care of himself, but I don't like people to talk about my kids.

COACH DAVID LUEKING (Austin): Janis tries to keep us aware of what is really important. She is the one who rattles the beds on Sunday morning and gets us out to church. She makes us do our parts around the house. She won't let us sit around the house in our tennis shoes all day long and watch basketball games.

Janis keeps our feet on the ground. If I have an exceptionally good ball game, she doesn't let me get too cocky. If Mark has a good game she reminds him to go pick up his socks or tells him, "You didn't do the dishes."

JANIS LUEKING (wife of David Lueking, mother of Mark Lueking): Our son Mark confides in me. I am his outlet. He tells me things and asks me not to tell his dad. It mainly is things he wants to get off his chest. If he is hurt or sick he will tell me, but he will ask me not to tell his dad. He doesn't want to miss a game.

BILL SHEPHERD (former Carmel coach, now Carmel athletic director): My wife was the one who had to sit there and listen to the fans gripe at my coaching and the two boys playing together. You don't really know what goes on in the stands until you quit coaching. After twenty-one or twenty-two years you are back in the stands and you understand what happens. You don't hear everything when you are coaching or maybe you can close your ears a little.

Edie was great and she deserves a lot of credit because she heard a lot of things from the people in the stands. A lot of them were good, in fact most of them were, but there are always negative people no matter what happens.

COACH DAN BUSH (Bedford-North Lawrence): Alan will tell my wife, Carol, a lot of things he doesn't tell me. I have no problems with that. There are times when I get on him and she will go in and soothe him.

RUTH SORRELL (wife of Mike Sorrell, mother of Ryan Sorrell): My role was one of support for both Mike and Ryan. I supported Mike and made sure he was fair to Ryan. Ryan sometimes thought his dad was harder on him than the other players. I tried to help Ryan understand that because Mike was harder on him, it would make it better for him as a result.

I let them both know that I was there if they needed me.

LINDA SLATON (wife of Coach Ron Slaton, mother of Marc Slaton): One night Marc came in and said, "You ought to divorce him [his dad] so we could move to another school system."

I said, "Marc, I'm also the coach's wife and if you don't like what he does, you'll just have to change."

Ron sat down and talked to him after that and smoothed things over before the next practice.

DONNA ALLEN (wife of Coach Herschell Allen, mother of Michael Allen): I wash a lot of uniforms for Michael and go to a lot of games. I love sports.

It has been a good situation for Herschell and Michael because the two of them get along well and there seldom is any friction between them. When

Herschell thinks Michael needs to improve on something, he approaches it positively. When Michael needs help, he will come to his dad for advice.

But it's not Utopia. *(Editor's note: Which might be too much to ask of any family involved in basketball 365 days a year.)*

JANET HART (wife of Coach Joe Hart, mother of Joey Hart): Sometimes it's difficult. Sometimes it's rewarding. I usually stand back and let things work themselves out.

Neither one likes to lose and sometimes there is a little friction over what they expect from each other. Those things usually work themselves out. They have a thirty-minute ride from Dugger to our home in Bloomfield, so that often gives them time to work out their disagreements.

Things seemed to get easier between Joey's sophomore and junior years.

Sometimes when they are not happy with each other, one of them will tell me his side, then the other will tell me his. That helps because at times they can only see from their own point of view. But I try to stay out of it as much as I can because I don't know the entire situation. I don't know what went on.

NANCY FORD (wife of Coach Jack Ford): When Ric was going through pushups as punishment, he told me that he was physically hurting. He said, "I think I'm going to quit. I think I'm going to quit the team, I can't take it."

I said, "What do you mean you can't take it?"

He said, "My body! My body cannot take any more of this."

I said, "Maybe if you'd start doing what you are supposed to do, you might not have to do those pushups. But you do what you have to do. If you feel you cannot handle that situation, then probably the best thing you can do is quit."

The next morning when he got up, I asked, "Well?" He said, "Oh, you knew I wouldn't do that. It's all right." And that was the last we heard of that.

They're on the Map

COACH JACK BUTCHER AND SONS BILL, BERNIE AND BOB

Some sportscasters can't pronounce it, some sportswriters can't spell it, and some Hoosiers don't know where it is, but it's on the map where US 50 and US 231 meet as they snake across Martin County's rolling terrain.

The road signs say it's Loogootee. The water tower proclaims "State Runner-up 1975" and "Coach of the Year — Jack Butcher—1970 and 1975."

Loogootee could be called "Butcherville," or "Jack's Place." Towns have been named for men who accomplished less than Jack Butcher. Basketball star at the high school in the early 1950s, a graduate of Memphis State, and an Army veteran, he's a hometown boy who came back to coach.

He became Loogootee's coach in 1957, and began building basketball teams and molding boys into men. In thirty-two years, through the 1988-89 season, Jack Butcher's Loogootee Lions won 592 times and lost only 163, giving him a winning percentage of .784, the best of any state coach who has been in the game more than three years.

He's also made Loogootee a familiar word in a basketball-crazy state. His 1970 team made it to the Final Four of the state tournament. His 1975 squad, led by son Bill, lost to Marion in the state championship game.

Around Loogootee, folks will tell you Jack Butcher is his own man. More than three decades of success can give a person a sense of independence.

Mention basketball and Jack Butcher is willing to talk, even on a break between classes. Butcher props up his feet on his desk in his gym office, lights up a cigar, breathes a sigh of relief, and says, "This is a good place to escape after two hours of driver education."

A good way to get most men talking is to ask about their sons. Jack Butcher is no exception.

Bill was his first son. He played for his dad before graduating in 1975. Bill is now a vice president for Merchants Bank in Indianapolis.

Second son Bernie played for his dad, graduated in 1980, and decided to become a basketball coach himself. After a three-year stint at South Knox he moved to Washington as head coach before the 1989-90 season.

Bob is a year younger. A 1981 Loogootee graduate, now he's an engineering technician at the Naval Weapons Support Center at Crane and coaches grade school.

Of Bill his dad says, "I think the first boy is very unique in everyone's family. I think parents, fathers in particular, may have aspirations for all their boys but I think they want the first in particular to be a good athlete.

"Bill was with me more than the other boys at a very early age. He came into the gym even before he could walk. Later on, he sometimes would hide in the car so he could come with me."

Bill Butcher got his start, like many other kids, by shooting the ball at a little goal in the house. "We would shoot a little nerf ball, or some other ball, and make a game out of it."

So it was natural progression, Jack Butcher said, for the other two boys to play the game.

Jack Butcher could tell almost from the beginning that Bill had natural talent for basketball. "We played a lot of basketball, of course, in and around the house. He was with me a great deal of the time and it was natural that he became interested in athletics. At the time, we had a swimming pool and he learned to swim at an early age. I think he just came up in an athletic type of environment. All those things help to develop coordination . . .

"I had a job that put all my sons in a situation where they were active and had access to sports. A lot of fathers work at jobs that are away from that kind of environment and they don't have the energy, or don't take the opportunity, to expose their sons to athletics.

"Parents have a very big role in whether a child will be interested in sports.

"That is true also from the standpoint of education. I think if parents show an interest in education at home the kids are generally going to have a very positive attitude about education. If parents will take the time to ask the kids about their grades and provide them the opportunity to study at home they will become pretty good students."

The Butcher boys didn't go to every varsity practice when they were young. Their studies came first. But Jack took them to the gym if they wanted, or if he had something to show them.

"I think just being exposed to practice is an advantage," Coach Butcher says. "I think if you are in the gym and observing things at a young age it's natural for you to develop an interest in the game, even though you aren't out on the floor."

The Butcher boys started playing organized basketball in the fourth or fifth grade, and father Jack watched their development through high school.

Jack Butcher stressed fundamentals—from shooting to defense to making the move to get open to shoot—not only to his sons, but to all players. Most of all, Butcher emphasized the need to be competitive.

Bill Butcher had to be competitive. "He not only had some very fine players in his class, he had great players both in front of him and behind him."

And Bill met the test. He had access to the gym and he worked hard on the fundamentals his dad stressed while he was there. He was a trailblazer of sorts. He was the first son in the area to play for his father.

"I think there was more pressure on him. I think it was more difficult for him than it was for the other boys because he was the first one to play for me," Jack Butcher says, looking back a decade.

Bill Butcher broke into the varsity starting lineup midway through his freshman year. He helped turn the team around; it went on to win the 1972 sectional and came close to winning the regional.

The Loogootee Lions had a golden era when Bill was in high school, capped by the march to Indianapolis and the state finals. The success of Bill and the '75 team made the way for Bernie and Bob a little easier. Fans had learned the Butcher boys knew basketball.

As an Indiana all-star and a member of the state finals team, Bill had been placed on a pedestal by the younger brothers. They wanted to follow the trail he had blazed. "It was just a natural thing," their father says. "Even though I may have spent more time with Bill at a very young age, the other boys were exposed to it almost as much . . . And they had a hero, an older brother to look up to, where he didn't have."

Two years after Bill Butcher graduated, Bernie joined the team. His father says he was very competitive, a good, very quick defensive player: "He wasn't a big scorer, and in his senior year he was relegated to being the floor leader. We had some pretty good kids inside, so his job was to set up the offense and get the ball to them.

"He wasn't as prolific a scorer as Bill or Bob, but nevertheless he could certainly play the game well."

While Bernie had to work harder at basketball, it came more naturally for Bob. Bob joined the varsity in 1978 and played two years with Bernie. He, too, was a solid defensive player, and he could shoot, once scoring 43 points in a game, for a time a Lions' Den record.

Loogootee returned to the semistate in 1981, when Bob was a senior.

"Bernie and Bob both were excellent ball players. Maybe they weren't the most popular kids in their classes, but certainly they got along well with their classmates and peer groups. I think that helps. They worked well as a team and they hustled, as did the entire squad."

Coach Butcher adds, "There was some unhappiness, but it was very minimal. You are always going to have somebody unhappy if you're playing your son in front of another player. I think it is really kind of remarkable that

Son Bernie Butcher (coach, South Knox) with dad, Bill, Loogootee coach

we had so little trouble."

A MOTHER'S ROLE: Jack Butcher credits his wife, Rita, with making sure their sons became well-rounded individuals.

"She provided the consistency they needed. She insisted that they have a period of study at home. We have four girls, in addition to the three boys, and she insisted that they do their homework as soon as they arrived home from school. School work had to be done before they were allowed to play.

"By the time Bernie was in high school he was studying before breakfast. Here again, things came natural for Bob and he didn't have to study hard, but he had that exposure to the other kids studying."

Butcher decided early on to separate basketball from the family's home-life.

"It is hard for people to believe, but we really didn't discuss basketball to any significant degree at home. When I thought it was necessary to talk to any of the boys about matters that pertained to the team, I took them to the gym and counseled them there."

Like most coaches, he dislikes losing: "If we lost, which fortunately wasn't often, I wouldn't be in the best of moods when I came home. Usually when I'm not in a very good mood, I'm silent anyway. So my wife didn't have to serve as a mediator among me and the boys.

"She no doubt, when I wasn't around, did some counseling on her own, advising the kids. They went to her before they came to Dad, anyway, for advice and guidance."

THE COACH-PLAYER RELATIONSHIP: Many coaches admit they are harder on their own sons than on other players. "I'm sure Bill would say that was the case," says Jack Butcher.

"I think it would be natural, and certainly more beneficial, to hold your son to a higher standard than other players. You certainly couldn't do the reverse.

"I don't think that coaches who have sons playing for them can treat them differently. At least they can't treat them better. That obviously would stick out like a sore thumb."

There are often allegations of favoritism when coaches put their sons in the lineup. Butcher admits such reactions are natural. "I feel that we, myself, the family, student body and the community as a whole, handled it just about as well as any situation around.

"I think one reason that it was handled as well as it was was because all three of my sons were pretty good players. I think most people, certainly in Indiana and here in Loogootee, are knowledgeable enough about the game that they know who are the better players.

"Most of the time a coach's son has to be not just a step better, but two or three steps better, than other players."

HIS GREATEST PLEASURE: Most players, Jack Butcher believes, have a good father-son relationship, even though their fathers may not be their coach. But the pride of fathers who coach successful sons may be greater.

"I suppose if I had to pick out one thing that gave me the greatest satisfaction it would be when we won the semistate in 1975 and went to the state finals. We had gone to the regional the four years I was in high school, but we never won the regional and never reached that dreamland of Sweet Sixteen.

"And so when my son did it for me, even though it was him doing it, I think in a way it was an extension of me. I was in the top 25 in the state, but I didn't make the Indiana All-Stars. Bill was an Indiana All-Star and that was probably the biggest highlight of all."

LOOKING BACK: Would Jack Butcher do it all over again? "We often think about our station in life," he says, "whatever job we might have. Basketball certainly has been very, very good to me and I probably would do it all over again."

BERNIE BUTCHER: Jack Butcher believes that his son Bernie's role as floor leader may have led him to coaching.

"He had a fundamental knowledge and interest in the game and not just the sporting aspect of it," his dad says.

The son adds, "I knew about the game just being around it. I had seen the good side and bad side. Being the son of a coach had prepared me for what to expect. I knew about the heartaches and disappointments that would occur. I knew what could happen and would happen."

One of those events occurred on December 16, 1988, when Coach Bernie Butcher's South Knox team pulled a major upset. It defeated his dad's unbeaten and highly-ranked Loogootee team, 68-67 in double overtime.

"It felt very good," Bernie Butcher remembers. "I thought we had a chance to beat them when the game went into overtime.

"Dad congratulated me. But when we got together as a family later, my brothers and sisters weren't quite sure what to say."

Jack Butcher remembers it as "a unique experience, having your son beat you. I was very happy for him. I was not very happy otherwise, because I didn't think we'd played particularly well. I don't think my disappointment was because he won the game, but because we didn't play well."

Jack Butcher took some razzing from his friends around Loogootee. "But I usually told whoever it was that next year is another year and there won't be any mercy. They'll be in my gym then."

That didn't turn out to be the case. Bernie Butcher left South Knox to coach Washington, Loogootee's archrival, a big step for a twenty-eight-year-old with three years of varsity coaching experience.

Bernie Butcher said the time he spent as a youngster around the gym gave him an opportunity to learn more about the game than other kids: "I thought I had to work harder because I was the coach's son."

BILL BUTCHER: Fifteen years after high school graduation, Bill Butcher's admiration for his father is still evident. "I liked to be around my dad when I was young. If he was mowing the grass, working in the garden, or going to the gym, I wanted to be there."

His father was a role model who not only taught him basketball but shaped his values.

"I had great admiration for my dad, not just because of basketball but all his other characteristics."

Bill was a gym rat who went to the gym almost every day. "Older kids, when dad wasn't around, called me 'Little Jack' or 'Baby Butch.' They'd never let my dad hear them call me that."

He remembers hiding behind the front seat of the car until his dad was almost to the gym. "Then I'd pop up and it'd be too late for him to take me back home. He would get mad at me for a while, but I'd do it again."

Sons of coaches feel pressure, but Bill Butcher said he thinks a lot of his was self-inflicted.

"There was a lot at stake for a family in a coaching situation, not only for the coach and player, but for every member of the family as well."

He remembers: "We talked about the situation and decided it was important to be successful if we were to go forward with the coach-son relationship. Doing it halfway would not be satisfactory."

Bill remembers some problems as early as the fourth or fifth grade. "There was some resentment and jealousy from families of older players when I was playing a grade ahead."

But the most critical time came when Bill was a freshman. "It was a very difficult time. I don't know for what reason, but I just wasn't performing on the freshman team. I did better on the JV team and in practice against the varsity I did even better.

"The higher the level of competition, the better I played. It was embarrassing. Dad and I sat down at the time and decided if the anxiety continued and it was a situation I couldn't get past, then I'd better walk away from it."

When you are about to have your tennis shoes hung up by your dad and coach it shocks you. Opposing coaches talked to Jack Butcher and told him, in effect, "To hell with the community, put the kid on the varsity."

Bill Butcher moved up halfway through his freshman year. By sectional time he was a starter.

Bill Butcher recalls being booed when he was introduced as a starter. "It was a toss-up whether the booing was louder from the opposition's fans or Loogootee fans. Dad got booed by the opposing fans, but not the home fans, so my boos were louder than his.

"We won the sectional and suddenly the fans who booed were my friends and the booing went away."

Because Bill played ahead of his classmates most of his career, he didn't develop close friendships on his teams, as Bernie and Bob did later.

"I was playing with seniors as a freshman, and some of the sophomores and juniors resented that. Neither Bernie nor Bob played as freshmen on the varsity, and that helped."

The early 1970s were golden years for Loogootee—state finalists in 1970 and 1975, final eight in 1971, six sectionals in a row.

ROARING LION: Let's let Bill Butcher relate this story in his own words:

"I rode on the team bus to the away games and it was a big deal for a kid in the second, third and fourth grades. I can still smell the Juicy Fruit gum that was passed out enroute to games.

"We were on the way home one night when some of the players started questioning me on the back of the bus. One of them asked, 'Say, Baby Butch, what does your dad say about me?'

"I told him something that was complimentary. Another player asked, 'And what does he say about me?' I gave him a neutral answer.

"When the third one asked me what Dad said about him I went into a dissertation about how bad he was. I told him everything Dad had said about him and none of it was good.

"The other players broke up. Dad heard the laughter, turned about and asked what was going on. It was the last time I got to ride in the back of the bus."

Bill Butcher went on to Hanover College, where he played for three years.

All in the Family

COACH JIM HAMMEL AND SONS CHIP AND RICHIE

It is November 1987 and Jim Hammel is still looking over the players who are candidates for his Lafayette basketball team. His son Chip is a freshman, but he hasn't made the team yet. The other players may be wondering how Chip, the player, will be treated by his dad, the coach.

It doesn't take them long to find out.

Suddenly, the coach kicks Chip out of the gym.

"Imagine that," recalls Jim Hammel. "He's the first guy in history to get kicked out of trials and he's my son." He no longer remembers why he ordered his son from the gym: "He probably didn't do something quickly enough. I may have been trying to show him that he couldn't get away with anything. I may have wanted to prove to the other players that Chip would be given no favors because he was my son. It may have been by design."

Chip made the junior varsity despite his brief exile. A year later, his brother Richie came on the scene as a freshman. When he didn't get booted out of practice Chip wondered whether his father had mellowed.

"He can't believe Richie hasn't been kicked out," Jim Hammel says, appearing to wonder somewhat himself:

"Chip is a very dedicated, very intense person. Richie is more of a free spirit. Chip thinks I've mellowed. He thinks that Richie doesn't have to go through the same things he had to go through."

Jim Hammel won't say whether he has softened. Maybe he had already made the point that all men who coach sons have to make: There will be no favoritism.

BROTHERS, TEAMMATES: Chip and Richie Hammel saw or played in many of the 306 games his father's teams had won as of the 1989-90 season.

"Chip sat beside me on the bench every game from the time he was about four years old, starting at Mooresville, through the eighth grade. I don't think he ever missed a practice, either at Mooresville, Lake Central, or here at Lafayette until the time he started playing junior high basketball," his dad recalls.

"Chip was a true gym rat. He was around it so much that he was able to really get an understanding of the game and what it takes to be successful."

Hammel calls Chip and Richie "two entirely different players, entirely different kids. Richie hasn't really had that same interest in doing what Chip did. He was content to sit on the second row with the team and wasn't as serious about it or as intent as Chip was."

Chip is a point guard and Richie is an off guard, a shooter. (Jim Hammel still has a son on the bench with him. When Chip moved onto the varsity as a freshman, third son Scott moved into the seat as a second grader. He comes to every practice.)

The gym was a good environment for the growing Hammel boys.

"I've had really good leaders," says their father. "I've had good kids that have set good examples for them, kids like Doug Opel and Jim Bagley at Mooresville and Milan Petrovic at Lake Central, a player who won the Trester Award when Lake Central went to the state finals in 1984.

"We came to Lafayette and they ran into Mark Jewel who was the 1986 Mr. Basketball. He is as nice a person as I've ever met in my life. He was a straight-A student.

"They have always had good role models, and it was easy to put them on a bus to games, let them come to practice, let them be in the locker room. You knew the things they were going to pick up would be positive."

The Hammel boys also picked up a lot of knowledge about the game on scouting trips. They still go at times.

"I point out things to them they can use or things we can use against the team we are scouting. I guess that's the coach in me, but when we're at a game or we're sitting at home watching TV I'm always asking them what they would do in certain situations. Some of that rubs off on them."

Both Chip and Richie started playing organized basketball in the first grade at Lake Central and they have been on teams ever since. After Chip's sophomore and Richie's freshman year, their dad wasn't sure when they might be better-than-average players, but "I could tell at a young age that they really had an interest. If a kid likes anything, he probably will have a chance to be pretty good at it."

Both boys have wide-ranging interests in athletics, and their dad approves. "I've told other kids on the basketball team that I want them to play other sports. I think it's really good for them . . . It's important for them to stay busy. There still is plenty of time for basketball."

Hammel's sons have kept busy, indeed. Chip, as a sophomore, won a varsity letter in football as a wide receiver. In basketball he was all-North Central Conference first team. In baseball he was a starting left-fielder and lead-off hitter.

Richie was a quarterback in football and won a varsity letter in basketball as a freshman.

And they are both outstanding students, taking advanced honors courses.

Lest they be labeled perfect, Jim Hammel says, "They don't always get honor grades all the time."

CHIP AND RICHIE, THE PLAYERS: Chip Hammel played on the Jayvee team as a freshman, then moved up to the varsity as a sophomore. His father admits, "I really didn't want to bring Richie up as a freshman, either. It was a very forced thing. We [Lafayette] were a horrible shooting basketball team and we not only needed depth, but someone who could score."

Richie was moved up two-thirds of the way through the season, after scoring about thirty points in a reserve game at East Chicago.

"We [Hammel and his assistants] decided on the way home it was time to bring him up because we didn't have anyone who could throw the ball in the ocean.

"He probably is the best shooter at his age I have ever coached. He's a pure shooter, although he doesn't do all the things Chip does."

Richie didn't start any varsity games as a freshman. His dad assesses his play as "decent, nothing spectacular." Richie had his good moments and his bad moments. Some good moments came the last game of the 1988-89 season when he scored 12 points in the second quarter and bailed his team out of a deficit to beat McCutcheon, a team Lafayette had lost to the year before.

But a huge disappointment at the sectional "is something I'm sure he'll never forget," says Jim Hammel. Lafayette was pitted against West Lafayette.

The clock showed 17 seconds left when Hammel's team, trailing by two points, got the ball out of bounds. The coach describes what happened: "We called a time-out. Our number-one shooter had fouled out. We decided to run a play that had a couple of options. One of the options was to reverse the ball to Richie and for him to take the shot if they sagged in on our big man. He took the shot and missed it. As a freshman, that's tough."

There is a lot of tradition in Lafayette, which seldom loses a sectional. "I know that has been a tough time for him," his dad understands. "It has been a tough time for all of us. But people here have been super," but he adds, "there were probably people who said he shouldn't have been there to take the shot.

"But to his credit he went out the next day, a Saturday, and played about three hours over at the Y and he has never stopped. He came to the gym at six o'clock in the morning before school and practiced and returned in the evening.

"To his credit, he didn't let it defeat him. Instead he let it drive him. He is reacting in a very positive way."

THE PRESSURES: Any successful coach will play the kids he believes will help him win. Jim Hammel plays his son Chip because "he's a real leader and as point guard he really takes charge." Richie plays because he's a scorer.

Jim Hammel says, "You're always going to catch flak any time you use younger kids and end up not having the team success that you want. We weren't bad [during the 1988-89 season], but we didn't win the sectional. We had been in the semistate all the other years."

THE FAMILY THAT PLAYS TOGETHER: Coach Jim Hammel with sons Chip (left), Richie (right), and Scott.

The result is some griping among fans. When it's the coach's kid, it's easier to point a finger and allege prejudice and favoritism.

Jim Hammel is a realist: "I can't say that anybody ever said that to me or that it has been vocal, but I'm sure it was there. I'd probably be the same way if I was a father and I had a kid that was a senior and they started a sophomore in front of him, or if a freshman played in front of my kid. Being a father, it's just a natural thing . . .

"I watch the baseball games and if [my own son] comes out of the game I can feel myself asking what is the coach doing. Later I say to myself, 'Thank God I didn't say anything.' I can feel it. I chafe at it.

"So I can see it from the other side. And it's tough.

"But I really believe as a coach you are going to play the guys that you think can help you win and you're not going to let that outside interference bother you."

Everyone learns from experience, and Jim Hammel picked up a few things from coaching his sons.

"I think I'll be a lot more aware of the feelings of other kids. It's easy for other kids to be hurt. I think one of the things you have to do as a coach of your son is to go out of your way to communicate with the other kids. It's a human reaction for a player to say the reason he isn't playing is because the kid ahead of him is the coach's son.

"Now that I've been through that for a year, I will spend more time soothing other players and doing a better job explaining their roles to them."

IN THEIR SHOES: Some thoughts from Jim Hammel:

"I'm not very fair to Chip and Richie. I'm the first to admit it. I wish I could say differently but I take it home and I'll end up yelling at them about something.

"We'll be watching a game and I'll say, 'Chip, now that's the same thing you're doing.' I get on them and I wonder if they ever get a chance to really relax.

"I can't say it has bothered them to this point.

"I wish I could leave it here in the gym.

"I know I'm a lot harder on them than anyone else in practice. There are times when you have to come down on a team and you decide to use someone as an example. Your sons are easy examples.

"But, again, they've handled that really well."

"There are times, no doubt about it, that I'd rather that they were playing for someone else. I think for their good they would be better off. And yet it's something I wouldn't want to give up. It's a one-time thing you are never going to have a chance to do again. But sometimes I wonder if it's best for them.

"They could be like every other kid. Now they have to obey every rule. They have to toe the line.

"For example, Chip forgot his shoes when he came to the gym for our trip to Kokomo and a big North Central Conference game. He runs home to get them. In doing so he's late getting on the bus. I'm not sure how I would have reacted to any other kid, but I suspended him for that game."

AT MEAL TIME, TOO: With a father as coach, two sons as players, Susie, a second-grade daughter, and Scott, a third-grade son, Sue and Jim Hammel rarely have time for a weekday meal together.

"On Sundays we always sit down and we try to keep a friendly atmosphere. But if the team didn't play well or the boys didn't play well that may be hard. But the sad part is basketball comes up in May, too, and I'll ask, 'What did you do today, Chip, to get better?' It's the off-season and I'm still on them about basketball."

SOME ADVICE TO OTHERS: So what advice would Jim Hammel give to a coach who has his son as a player for the first time?

"I think, more than anything, you need to pray that they are either going to be outstanding or terrible. As long as a player is above average he'll create no problem for his father. If he is very poor, he won't be playing that much. It's the average player who will get the most criticism.

"I think my sincere advice would be to enjoy it. Realize that it's a one-time thing.

"My two sons are playing and they happen to be playing together and for me. Whether they play or not play it's a special time because I'm with them. I really love these two kids. I really cherish that time we have together.

"Whether they have individual success or not is beside the point, but, hopefully, we'll have very great teams the last two years they play together."

Looking back, looking forward, Coach Hammel, would you want to coach your son Scott when he reaches high school?

"I would say I would not be against it. Scott is always talking about that time. So, yes, I think I would want to coach him."

An Early Start

COACH DAVID LUEKING AND SON MARK

Freshman Mark Lueking was knocked unconscious in a collision with another player in Austin's game with Salem in the 1988-89 season. Mark's dad, Dave Lueking, looked on from the opposite end of the court.

"I had attended to many injured players in twenty-four years as a coach," Lueking says, "but that was the first time I really got a taste of coaching my son. Before I had just been a coach on the floor. I hadn't considered myself his dad in practice or at games.

"My concern as a parent came out that night and it was a feeling I hadn't had before. He was really hurt and I was very concerned for him."

Mark Lueking was out for about thirty minutes after rolling over and asking for his dad. Taken in an ambulance to the hospital, he was diagnosed as having a serious concussion. He was out of action for several days but returned to the starting lineup and finished with some exceptional statistics for a freshman: 11.8 points, 5 assists, 3-½ steals and 4 rebounds per game.

"We've had some outstanding freshmen play here and I thought, by comparison, he did well," his dad said.

BEGINNINGS: Mark Lueking became a gym rat as soon as he could walk. His dad and his mother, Janis Lueking, thought when he was a year old that he may have taken up residency in the gym.

Austin had played Scottsburg in an exciting game. When Coach Lueking got up about 3:00 a.m. to check on Mark he was gone from his bed. The Luekings searched the house over and couldn't find him.

"We decided, in our excitement at the game," Coach Lueking recalls, "that we had left him at the gym. We were about ready to leave for the gym when we thought to look under the bed. We found Mark there.

"I thought for a while I had lost my son after I had him for only a year."

A neighbor built Lueking an adjustable goal when Mark was a toddler. "I slid it down to seven feet, bought a goal with a reduced rim, and Mark started shooting layups and free throws," Coach Lueking recalls.

"I think that helped him get his start. He learned to be successful and he learned to do it the way I asked him to. With a bigger basket and a bigger ball he might have developed some bad habits that would still be haunting him."

Young Lueking always played ahead of his class. As a kindergartener he performed with fourth graders.

The family moved to Tell City from Austin when Mark was a first grader, and he played with fifth and sixth graders there. Coach Lueking noticed early his son had good quickness and good hands.

"I thought if he was interested in the game he would be a good player."

These expectations became realities when Mark scored 18 points as a first grader in a scrimmage against fifth-grade students.

Mark wore a sports coat and tie to high school games, just like the players did, and sat on the bench as a toddler.

And, as all kids are, he was impressionable. Steve Alford has always been one of Mark's idols. But when he was younger he idolized players on his dad's teams, with curious results:

"A couple of those heroes got hurt in games. I spent a year and a half trying to get it out of Mark's mind that when he dribbled down the floor he wasn't supposed to fall down and get hurt.

"He'd fall down and say he had a bad ankle and a bad knee, then he'd get up, shake it off and go shoot like they would. It's funny how kids sometimes pick up certain aspects of the game. At that point in life, he thought you were supposed to get hurt."

So how much did Mark pick up just being around the gym? His dad responds:

"He understands and he sees a lot of things. He has watched the older kids. When he was younger he used to stand behind me during games with his hands on my shoulders. When we stood up at time-outs, he'd be standing inside the huddle looking up at all of us.

"I finally put him to work, trying to keep him busy, letting him be the ball boy. Then I let him handle the water bottles, and then I let him be a statistician's assistant."

When Mark was an eighth-grade statistician Dave Lueking learned what other parents have learned: they sometimes don't hear what their kids tell them.

"Mark had been telling me he wasn't seeing very well. He was doing the stats in a game against Salem and I heard him ask someone, 'What's that boy's number?' I got up and said, 'Mark, what are you talking about?' He said, 'Dad, I've been telling you for six months I can't see.' We took him to Louisville the next day and, sure enough, he needed glasses."

The lack of glasses hadn't stopped Mark from seeing the basket, though. In the sixth grade he averaged 31 points a game, 30 in the seventh, and 28.9 as an eighth grader. As a grade-schooler he had several games his dad often

MUTUAL ADMIRATION: Austin freshman starter Mark Lueking with his dad, Austin Coach David Lueking

wished he could have saved until high school.

"We had played Jeffersonville at Austin when Mark was a seventh grader and beat them by about 28 points. We went down to Jeff when Mark was an eighth grader and a big crowd showed up because both teams were unbeaten."

Jeff fans chanted, "Okay, Lueking, we're not in Austin. Your dad isn't going to be able to protect you tonight." Mark scored 48 points in that game and had about twenty rebounds and ten assists, even though his team lost 69-66.

After that junior high career, it was natural for Dave Lueking to think about playing his son on the varsity as a freshman. He recalls the factors he considered: "His ability entered into it more than anything else. I wanted to make sure he was going to play at the varsity level. I wanted to make sure he fit in with our guards and the people we had.

"We let him come in and get his feet on the ground without putting a lot of pressure on him. The sixth game was against New Washington, which featured the Matthews twins, who also were coached by their dad, and Shannon Arthur.

"We were down about 18 points and I put Mark in the game. He scored 18 points while holding one of the twins to nine while he was in the game.

"After that, we decided he was ready for a starting spot."

Five-feet-ten as a freshman, Mark played both guard positions, but his dad thinks his best spot is at the point.

HOW FANS FEEL: Some coaches are criticized when they move their freshman sons into the varsity lineup. Coach Lueking's experience was different.

"I had more people who wanted him to start earlier than later. A lot of people asked me before the seventh ball game why I wasn't starting him. I really wanted to take some of the burden off of him and give him a chance to get adjusted."

GREAT EXPECTATIONS: Like other fathers who coach their sons, Dave Lueking was sometimes harder on Mark than on the other players: "I think I was harder on Mark than I may have needed to be. We sometimes expect perfection out of our own sons. We are more impatient with them than other players."

Other players recognized that. Mark told his mother one night after he had been criticized by his dad that the other players rated his effort a 9 on a scale of 10. Some of them even invited him to stay with them if the coach got too rough on him. Coach Lueking, however, never got that hard on player Lueking.

Austin was at Eastern (Pekin), which was led by Noel Anderson, a 6'3" guard who had been a four-year starter. Before the game, Lueking, the coach, told Lueking, the player, that Anderson was a good ball player with great quickness. "You'll have to watch your passes," he advised.

"Mark's first pass of the game was intercepted by Anderson. I took Mark out and exiled him to the last seat on the bench, telling him to think it over and let me know when he was ready to play.

"Some of the kids down on the bench with him offered him some moral support at that time, too."

Overall, Lueking terms his son's first year a success: "He seemed to pick up things fairly quickly. He recognized defensive changes and adjusted on the court. He needs to continue to grow and mature and communicate with the other players in order to help make them better. I hope we can work it out so the team can take advantage of his experience and knowledge of the game. We've got other kids who can play, too, and he has to learn to fit in with their concept of the game."

IN SCHOOL: The son of a teacher-coach has to be a role model in school. Dave Lueking assesses his son's position: "I think everybody watches him. If he gets in trouble in school, which he doesn't very often, there is a lot of talk about it. He is under pressure not only from being a coach's son but for being a teacher's son. It's like being the son or daughter of a minister. People are constantly watching what he does and how he acts."

SOME ADVICE: Dave Lueking's advice for a coach who has a son as a player for the first time: "Develop a relationship as the son grows up where you understand each other. I think a coach has to convince his son he loves him. There are a lot of pressures that don't exist for other fathers and sons.

"I'm going to get up in front of three thousand fans at times and chew him out. I don't know of any other father-son relationship where a father chastises his son in front of an audience. And I don't know where any other father puts down his son before his peers as coaches do in practice.

"That son may be doing all he possibly can and you're insisting he do more. He ends up in front of his teammates being criticized in a manner that they aren't. You try not to do that and you try to keep it fair, but you can't get away from it."

What advice would he have for a son who is playing for his father for the first time?

"He has to be thick-skinned not only with his father, but with the other kids in school and the other players.

"He has to listen. He has to be a leader.

"Boys who play for their fathers must keep their mouths shut. If they need to reflect about basketball they need to do it with someone they can trust. They need to air some of their feelings. I think they need to learn where they can say things and to whom they can say them.

"They have to learn to keep secrets. If they hear their father talking about adjustments that are going to be made on the team, they can't talk about it. They are going to have to hear things, then forget them."

GROWING PAINS: Mark asked after his freshman season what he could do to improve and his dad told him, kiddingly, "You can grow before next season."

"Mark is at the point where I give him more advice on attitude than about skills. Being a fifteen-year-old freshman today is very difficult. I'm just trying to help him understand himself.

"My high school coach, Gunner Wyman, told me that the most difficult thing in life is being a parent and that you don't get to do it again.

"Mark is going through the time in his life which we can never go back and correct.

"I want him to a happy, well-rounded, adjusted child. I'd like for him to play in the band and to love music. I'd like for him to go to concerts and plays and have the opportunity to be all the things he would like to be.

"My wife, Janis, keeps that in the front of our minds, that basketball is not all we should be thinking about."

One of the things Mark Lueking thinks about are his grades. He finished his freshman year with a perfect 4.0 grade index.

DAD AND DAUGHTER: Dave and Janis Lueking have an elementary-school-age daughter, Mandy, who also has shown proficiency in basketball. And she has basketball fever, just like brother Mark. "It's a disease," Dave Lueking says. "It has gotten into their blood."

She, too, plays above her age level and her skills are obvious to her dad, who recalls: "I conducted a clinic at Hanover and called Mandy out on the floor to run a series of drills when she was a fifth grader. There were 150 boys watching and she was hitting every shot and dribbling left-handed. She had complete control of the situation."

Mandy feels, at times, that she doesn't get enough attention from her father. "She thinks I don't give her the attention that she deserves because I'm with Mark so much. Mark rides to the high school with me and he's there with me at the gym until 8:00 p.m. and he goes scouting a lot with me.

"My relationship with my daughter is one I have had to concentrate on so that she doesn't lose the fact that I love her in a very special way. I kid her all the time. If I had one wish, I tell her, it would be that she didn't play basketball, that she just be my daughter, that she wear dresses and be beautiful and that I could love her for all the things a father loves his daughter."

COACH OR DAD? Mark Lueking has always called his dad "Coach" at the gym. "This year he walked by a couple of times in the gym and said, 'How are things doing, Dad?' And I replied, 'I'll dad you.'

"But he did well in front of others. I was afraid he wasn't going to talk to me in high school. I thought it might be one of those relationships where he wouldn't acknowledge me. Being a teacher with a son in school was something to which I had to adjust."

FROM STEVE TO MARK: Mark had always idolized Steve Alford. When Mark went from the eighth grade into high school, Steve took time out from pro ball to write Mark that it was a special thing for a son to play for his dad. He wrote that he enjoyed the experience with his father, Sam, and that he was sure Mark would, also. He encouraged young Lueking to savor the four years because the time would pass quickly.

"I also talked with Sam Alford. And we watched the Matthews twins grow up at New Washington and we've stayed close to them. I coached with Gunner Wyman when his son played. So we have had some good advice about father-son, coach-player relationships," Dave Lueking says.

THE FUTURE: Dave Lueking knows, as most coaches do, that fans could become disenchanted with him even though they have always been supportive in the past.

"Our community is not going to accept losing. If we lose, it will find somebody to blame," Lueking asserts, though his teams have won two sectional titles and a regional.

"I'd hate to leave. I'd like to see Mark have an opportunity to finish what we started here.

"We like to be successful whether Mark is on the team or not. But with him, it will be extra-special."

Hoosier Basketball, Ohio Style

COACH ALAN DARNER AND SON LINC DARNER

Once a basketball game begins, a coach's son is just another player to his dad. Coaches must focus on the entire team, not just their sons.

Alan Darner, the Anderson Highland coach, has to. But sometimes it's difficult, especially when your son scores 35, 35, 53, 40, and 37 points in a five-game run that leaves nets in central Indiana burning.

His son Linc did that midway through his junior year in the 1988-89 season. His dad enjoyed those performances, but he wasn't as aware of his son's exploits as if he'd been a father in the stands.

"In the stands as a parent," he explains, "you are focusing on your son or daughter. As a coach, you have to see the entire floor."

Nevertheless, he had to feel a tinge of pride when his 6'4" son went on one of the hottest shooting streaks in years in Indiana. A few fans wondered if the coach had changed his offense. He hadn't. It was the one he had used for years. Young Darner ran the point in Highland's motion offense, learned to get open, and gained confidence when his shots started falling.

After a highly-successful career in Ohio, Alan Darner had come to Anderson three years earlier in search of Hoosier basketball mystique. He found it. And he and his son added another chapter to the saga of the sport.

LINC DARNER, THE PLAYER: Linc Darner started out as many sons of coaches do: a hoop lowered within his shooting range, a smaller ball, and a father who would give him instructions.

Linc—his name from a character in the TV show "Mod Squad"—started shooting at age four or five at a goal six and a half feet off the ground. From his dad, the coach, he learned the correct shooting form. When he was strong enough, the hoop was raised to eight feet.

In Medina, Ohio, where Darner coached, the goal was at eight feet for eight-year-olds, nine feet for nine-year-olds and ten feet for ten-year-olds. And players shot a smaller ball, similar to what is used in girls' basketball.

Like other coaches, Alan Darner thinks youngsters can learn too many bad habits trying to shoot a regulation basketball at a ten-foot hoop before they learn the proper techniques.

Linc Darner not only played the game when he was young, he studied it. He was around varsity practices at the schools in Ohio where his dad coached and picked up the offensive and defensive patterns. At home, later, he would draw up the offense on paper.

He started to go scouting when he was about eight and his dad would explain the defenses and offenses the teams were using. It was the same at football games, because in Ohio football is a bigger sport than basketball.

Linc started playing organized basketball when he was eight, and by that time he knew more about both football and basketball than others his age and played in elementary school with kids older than he was. As a fourth grader, for example, he played on the seventh-grade team.

By that time, his dad knew he could be a good basketball player. Fundamentally he was ahead of other boys his age, and he had worked on using both hands.

Darner, the player, entered Anderson Highland as a freshman when his dad took over as varsity coach. He bypassed the freshman team and played point guard with the junior varsity, where he was one of the top three players even though he carried only 125 pounds on a 5'11" frame.

Highland was loaded with upperclassmen, and as a sophomore Linc didn't crack the starting lineup on a team that went 18-3. But his dad credits him with igniting the team in several games. In the second contest, against tough Marion, Linc came off the bench, playing well and adding some scoring punch at guard.

Before the next game, against Madison Heights, a woman asked Alan Darner if Linc Darner was his son. Told he was, she asked, "Why don't you play him more?"

It was a positive reaction, a coach, and a father, likes to hear. The woman saw a lot more of Linc Darner that season in his relief roles on one of Highland's greatest teams.

And she saw much more of him in in the 1988-89 season when he became a starter . . . and a standout. He averaged 26.5 points a game, about thirty after mid-season. He had 3 assists a game and was the team's leading rebounder with 5.5 boards a game. On defense he was given the opposition's best scorer.

College scouts started streaming into gyms to see young Darner play. He gave a verbal commitment to join the Purdue Boilermakers for the 1990-91 season.

PRESSURE: "I didn't put any more pressure on Linc than I have on some of our better players over the years whom I thought were keys to our team. You tend to put more pressure on your better players because you expect more out of them," Coach Darner explains.

*HE LEFT THE NETS BURNING: Anderson Highland's Linc Darner
with his dad, Coach Alan Darner*

It is easy to understand that. If the top scorer averages 20 points a game, then scores 8 in a game, you stand a good chance of getting beat. That's a fact of life.

Linc Darner says he sometimes is used as an example in practice. "Come to one of our practices and you'll realize I'm the one who gets yelled at the most." That's normal, he says, for the leading scorer and the captain. It's not necessarily because he's the coach's son.

Pressure also comes from the fans' great expectations. When Linc Darner was on his 1988-89 shooting rampage, fans figured it was normal for him to score in the 30s. One mentioned to Coach Darner after one game that Linc hadn't had a good outing. All he had done was score 27 points despite being double-teamed the entire game.

In a sectional game, Linc scored 17 points and pulled down 13 rebounds. Again some fans said he didn't have a good game. At least 95 percent of the players in the state would have settled for that performance.

Some people, including sports writers and announcers, assume when a coach's son scores more than other players, the offense has been set up to get him the shots. That's not necessarily true, Alan Darner says.

"I've run the same offense for about fourteen years. I've had other kids that scored a lot of points off the same offense and no one implied I was doing something special for them. But when it's your son the implication is that you have designed an offense that will let him score.

"If you have a player who can score, you want him to get more shots whether he's your son or whether he isn't your son." The objective is to win with the personnel you have.

Coach Darner figures 98 percent of the fans are supportive; there are a few who will be critical no matter what.

FAMILY AFFAIR: For Alan and Diane Darner, basketball is more than a family affair. It's almost a way of life.

Linc isn't the only star in the family. Their oldest daughter, Amy, was a statistician for the team. Another daughter, Kim, had an outstanding two-year career at Anderson Highland. She played on the 1987 team that lost in the state championship, and was named to all-tournament teams in the sectional, regional, semistate and state finals that year.

Alan Darner admits, "I was more nervous sitting in the stands when Kim played than I am on the bench when Linc is playing and I'm coaching."

Kim started at guard at Indiana State as a freshman and was chosen team captain her sophomore season. Waiting in the wings, is brother Tige, an eighth grader (1989-90) who also shows good promise. Tige is two inches taller than Linc was at that age and appears to have as much ability, if not more, than his big brother. So it is natural that the Darners talk basketball at home.

"I probably should just go home and not talk about the game, or if I do, not bring up anything negative," he explains. "Sometimes I choose that time at home to mention what Linc should have done better in certain situations.

"If it was some other player I would talk to him in the gym or in my office. That's what I should do with Linc. If I do talk to him about basketball at home it should be as a father and not as a coach."

Mrs. Darner thinks her husband may be too negative on Linc at times. Those are the times she has to be real positive, a role Darner stresses other parents should play. In the preseason meeting he advises parents: "Let me handle the coaching and the criticism. You be positive when your son comes home after a game."

If Coach Darner is negative at home, Linc hasn't noticed it. He says, "On the basketball court, he's my coach. When I go home he's my father. If we do talk about what went on during a game or at practice things get back to normal in a short time."

Some players on the team, Linc Darner says, have to listen to their parents go on and on about the game. "We go home and we talk about it maybe for fifteen to twenty minutes and that's it," he says.

THE WORK ETHIC: Alan Darner has some advice for fathers who may be disturbed if their sons aren't stars in sports. He observes they can still be successful in life. Darner had one player who seldom got in the game, but he worked hard both at practice and in the classroom and became a doctor. Another player who rarely played remained on the team because of his work ethic and because he was a good student. He became an excellent lawyer.

"Hard work, at practice and at school, will carry over into a player's adult life, whether he becomes a minister, a teacher, a bricklayer, truck driver, or whatever," Darner adds.

"You would be surprised at how many former players have told me that the best thing that they learned when they played basketball was the work ethic. That makes coaching worthwhile."

LEARNING BY DOING: As a young coach with four youngsters, Alan Darner had no extra money for a blacktop driveway. It was gravel, instead. As the coach looks back, he thinks that may have been a big advantage. The ball didn't bounce true and Linc and Kim learned finger tip-control, which may have made them better ball-handlers.

Kids don't always need a gym to become good players. If there is a goal nearby, they can go out and shoot, shoveling off snow if necessary.

"You don't need glass backboards and a wooden floor to become a basketball player," says Alan Darner.

A LITTLE ADVICE: Now that Linc Darner has played for his dad, what advice would he give to his younger brother?

"I'd tell him, and other players whose dads are coaches, to never listen to what other people say about you.

"You should go out and work hard. If you are good enough you will have more fans cheering than are not cheering for you. Don't listen to the four or five people who want to talk about you. Listen to the two thousand who will say good things about you."

THE FUTURE: If Linc Darner could start his high school career over, he'd choose his dad as coach.

"It has been great. I wouldn't change it for any thing. If I had to do it over again, I'd want him as my coach all through high school."

After three years as Linc's coach, does Alan Darner want to coach Tige?

"Yes, I'd like coaching him. There are a lot of positives." And, he could have added, a lot of pleasures.

Leaving It in the Gym

COACH JACK FORD AND SON RIC FORD

It is a thin line, that divider between father-son and coach-player. Jack Ford said he drew that line and kept son Ric on one side, player Ric on the other.

"Once we left the gym floor, we didn't talk basketball. We had an agreement we kept. On the way home if I mentioned something about basketball he would remind me of that. If he brought something up, I would remind him."

Coach Ford had been around the game enough to know coaching his son wouldn't be easy. And he had talked with a number of coaches who had been through the experience.

Most agreed he should be careful to keep Ric from becoming a second-class citizen on the basketball court. If he deserves to play, he should be allowed to do so, they concurred.

Jack Ford agreed with that consensus. "I had always used the best players, regardless of what side of the tracks they were from. I was not going to make an exception just because Ric was my son."

Jack Ford also learned there were few coaches who had not heard their sons booed. Neither he nor Ric would be exceptions.

"It irritates you when you hear it. You have to block that out. He blocked it out, didn't let those things bother him and became a tougher person because of it," Coach Ford said.

Some allegations of favored treatment are absurd. One New Albany fan said the reason Ric led the state in steals as a senior was because his dad was the coach. But if there is any category a coach can't rig to favor his son, it's steals.

Another fan said Ric was valedictorian of his high school class because he was the coach's son.

Ric Ford also remembers the reactions of some overly-critical fans: "It was a no-win situation. If I played poorly they said the only reason I was playing was because I was the coach's son. If I played brilliantly, it wasn't enough to please them.

"There will always be some people you won't please, no matter how well you do. But my teammates helped. They told me not to worry when I was booed."

"I sort of worried about the booing the first couple of games, but after I realized my teammates understood the situation and were on my side it didn't bother me."

His dad adds, "If Ric scored 20, some people thought he should have scored 25, if he scored 25, they thought he should have scored 30."

THE POSITIVES: As in most father-son cases, there were more positives than negatives for Jack and Ric Ford.

Says Jack Ford, "One of the sad things about coaching is that you sometimes spend more time with other fathers' sons than you do your own. By coaching Ric, I had a rare opportunity to be with my son. Most fathers are working and trying to earn money to make ends meet and and can't be with their sons.

"Ric went scouting with me a lot. One night we made a trip from New Albany to Noblesville [260 miles roundtrip] to see two teams. Trips like that let our friendship as a father and son grow and develop. I was with my son during those years when he was a sophomore, junior, and senior and I relished that.

"I'm not saying we always agreed, but I think it was more than a father-and-son type of situation. Even now, when he wants some advice, he will call me."

Says son Ric Ford, "In high school I always knew what Dad wanted. In college [Atlanta's Oglethorpe University], I sometimes wasn't sure what the coach wanted.

"If I had my high school career to do over, I'd still want to play for my dad. There were a few bad points but I loved it."

As a senior at New Albany in 1984, Ric was valedictorian and an academic all-state basketball player. He went on to be an academic all-American at Oglethorpe.

THE MAKING OF A PLAYER: Ric Ford started playing organized basketball in the first grade. Jack Ford was coaching at Madison-Grant, near Marion, at the time, and Ric played in the Police Athletic League at Marion.

James Blackmon, who had been featured in *Sports Illustrated's* "Faces in The Crowd" section after scoring 40 points in a game, was on one of the teams. Ric Ford was assigned to guard him, an order he accepted with both excitement and reservation. He asked his father what he should do. He was told to always stay to his right.

The first time Blackmon got the ball he went right and beat Ric with his quickness. Ric came back down the floor, looked at his father and said, "I know, Dad. I know."

(James Blackmon was an Indiana All-Star in 1983 and played at the University of Kentucky.)

When Coach Ford later moved to Boonville, Ric played as a third and fourth grader on fifth and sixth grade teams. When his dad coached at Elkhart Ric played grade school ball there.

Jack Ford didn't have to encourage his son to play the game. "Ric always bugged me. I didn't have to bug him. He'd say, 'Let's go out and shoot some baskets.' We always worked with various phases of the game. I remember telling him at Boonville that he would never be a good player unless he could go both right and left. He was working on that as early as the fourth grade."

The Fords often worked together in the gym, but Ric also practiced a lot at an outside goal. It was quicker to go outside and shoot baskets than to go to the gym.

Ric played football and baseball and ran track in junior high, but decided to concentrate on basketball when he reached high school.

IN HIGH SCHOOL: When the freshman coach at New Albany suggested Ric Ford be moved up to the varsity, Jack Ford declined. "I just didn't want to push him too fast."

Ric Ford and another freshman dressed for the junior varsity games late in the season and Coach Ford noticed some testiness even then. "You could tell then he was the coach's son. It was a tense situation."

Ford did make the varsity as a sophomore, but was not a starter. Near the end of the season, he broke a finger during the Hoosier Hills Conference championship game against Bloomington North after coming off the bench to make some key steals.

Jack Ford acted like a coach instead of a father when that happened. "I don't remember saying this, but my wife swears I did. She insists I said, 'It was a good thing it was Ric instead of Bubby.'" (Bubby Mukes had the single-season scoring record for New Albany).

It was an unusual break that required surgery and a cast. Ric kept asking, "When am I coming back? When am I coming back?"

He dressed for the championship game of the sectional but was told he could not play. Jeffersonville, however, had a player who seemed to be hitting every shot he tried. Jack Ford kept asking, "Who can stop this kid? Who can go in there and stop him?"

A fearless sophomore, Ric volunteered. "I'll do it. I'll do it," he yelled.

Jack Ford, forgetting his son's injury in the heat of battle, replied, "Well, go in and do it." When Louie Jensen, Ford's assistant, reminded him about the injury, Coach Ford answered, "Well, he's in now. We'll have to take a chance with him." Ric stole the ball from the hot-shooter and New Albany came back to knot the score.

Then, Jack Ford says, came some smart coaching. "I took Ric out. His mother was really upset. She was up there, probably, screaming about an inconsiderate father who would play a son with a broken hand."

Jeffersonville took the lead again. New Albany got the ball out of bounds with one second to go and tried an alley-oop pass to Mukes. The ball went past Mukes' hands into the basket. The officials ruled that ball didn't touch Mukes' hands and disallowed the basket.

Jack Ford still wonders what would have happened had he left Ric in the game.

Ric was a starter his last two years in high school, playing off guard as a junior, point guard as a senior.

His statistics as a senior were good enough to earn him all-state honorable mention by both the Associated Press and United Press International. He averaged 12 points per game, 7 assists, and 8 rebounds, and led the state in steals.

RIC'S DEDICATION: Ric Ford was dedicated to the game. In high school, he got up in the morning on his own and did some running and shooting before breakfast. He'd grab a bite to eat, shoot some more, then lift weights. He played in the gym or at the park in the evening, which meant he worked out five to six hours a day.

ALL-AMERICANS: New Albany's Ric Ford with dad Jack Ford

Jack Ford said his son made up for what physical abilities he lacked by desire. "He was one of the hardest-playing kids I ever coached, even if that does sound like I'm bragging. He proved he deserved a spot on the team."

Ric Ford was a gym rat because that's where he preferred to be. "I went down to Indiana University Southeast and shot around a lot because the gym was always open. In the summer, I played every day except Thursdays and Fridays, and I would have played then if I had known where to get in a gym."

MIND GAMES: A lot of coaches are rougher on their sons than other players, possibly as a psychological move. It is one way to make sure other players accept them, to let it be known a son will get no special favor from his father.

But that's not the only reason, Jack Ford asserts.

"You are rougher because you expect more out of your son. I think that is why coaches' kids often end up being good players. It is demanded that they know the game."

Ric Ford has a confession. "I probably worked harder—don't tell my dad this—between my freshman and sophomore years than I did later on. I knew that there would be more pressure and I'd have to prove myself. I knew it had to be done then."

Ric realized his dad, whom he called "Coach" at the gym, was harder on him in practice than he was other players. "There was a point my senior year where we didn't get along very well. I remember running a lot of extra windsprints after practice. It was difficult for a couple of weeks and we finally had it out and I walked home rather than ride with him. I think much of what he did was to show the other players there wasn't any favoritism toward me."

LEARNING FROM EXPERIENCE: Jack Ford has some advice for sons who might play for their fathers:

"When you step out on that floor, son, you are a reflection of your father. Anything you do is going to reflect on him. Play hard and play to the best of your ability. Don't make a fool out of yourself. Don't let any physical actions on the floor reflect adversely on your school or on your dad.

"I can honestly say Ric never did anything to embarrass me."

FATHERS AND SONS: But he also adds, "Sons of coaches sometimes take on the burdens of their fathers. When things don't go right for the team, the son may feel it is his fault and accept too much of the blame."

When Jack Ford thinks about fathers and sons his mind turns to a song he has heard and the story it relates. In essence, it's a story of a young boy who asks his dad to play. The father replies, "I'd like to, Son, but I don't have time right now."

Time passes, the boy grows up. The father asks his son to join him in some endeavor. The son responds, "I'd like to, Dad, but I don't have time right now."

Time passes quickly. It's important that fathers and sons spend time together.

Ric Ford lives in Atlanta now and works as an actuary. The summer of 1989 was his first away from home.

"I'm thankful," Jack Ford concludes, "I had that opportunity a lot of fathers don't have when their sons are growing up."

DESIGNATED SPECTATOR: Nancy Ford, Jack's wife and Ric's mother, calls herself a "designated spectator." Jack Ford said she was more than that. "She was a stabilizing influence."

Being a spectator isn't easy. The complaints she heard in the stands about Jack didn't bother her. "That's part of the game," she admits. "But when fans start yelling at the players, that bothers me. The kids are out there playing as hard as they can."

At New Albany, a couple Mrs. Ford didn't know sat in the seats behind her criticizing Ric, then Jack. Nancy Ford fumed, but kept quiet.

The next game they were there again, complaining about the players and the coach. Tired of the complaints after a time, Nancy Ford turned and asked the couple, "If things are so bad, why did you come to the game?"

She had second thoughts, turned back to the disgusted fans, and apologized, explaining, "You bought tickets and you have a right to complain. But if you are so miserable why are you here? Why waste your money?"

The couple never sat behind Mrs. Ford again.

DAUGHTER JILL: Jack Ford was a tough taskmaster with Ric, and he didn't give his daughter, Jill, much slack, either. Jill, an Indiana University student after graduating fifth in her high school class, played girls' basketball at New Albany.

She once complained after a game because her coach had taken her out. Jack Ford told her, "Young lady, he kept you in the game a lot longer than I would have."

Jill stormed off to her mother, who once again was the buffer, this time between daughter and dad.

Postscript: Jack Ford coached at Washington after leaving New Albany. He also coached at Brook (now South Newton), Leesburg (now part of Warsaw), Lowell, Madison-Grant, Boonville, and Elkhart Memorial. He was assistant coach at the University of Louisville when the Cardinals won the NCAA championship in 1985. His teams won 329 games.

The Best Years of Their Lives

COACH TOM OLIPHANT AND SON JEFF OLIPHANT

Drive south out of Lyons on Ind. 67, look off to the right on a knoll, and you'll see a school with a quonset-type roof over the gym. To a nonbasketball fan, it's just another Indiana high school amidst the rolling farmland of southwestern Indiana.

To a basketball addict, it's L&M, a long-time consolidation that outlived a cigarette by the same initials. It brought the communities of Lyons and Marco together in 1959, and twenty-five years later created one of the great chapters in the storied history of Indiana high school basketball.

Lyons and Marco, two towns little noted nor long remembered by motorists enroute to Vincennes to the south or Indianapolis to the north. Two communities whose total population would not add up to 900 and where economic conditions are seldom bullish.

That would change in 1983 when Tom Oliphant's basketball Braves began chalking up victory after victory on the basketball floors of Greene County.

Tom Oliphant was a former star at L&M himself, graduating in 1964 before going on to Indiana State. His dad, Paul, had coached Indiana high school basketball, but at other schools.

Tom Oliphant had paid his coaching dues as an assistant coach at Union-Dugger and Worthington and as a head coach at Worthington and was in his first year at L&M.

He had brought more than his basketball knowledge to L&M. He had brought his son, Jeff, a husky, durable 6'5" player who had worked at the game ever since he learned to hold a basketball. Jeff had proved he could play the game as a freshman and sophomore at Worthington.

At L&M he would be playing with Tony Patterson and other juniors, who knew, too, how to play the game. Jeff Oliphant had no trouble blending in with Patterson and his pals. They finished the regular season undefeated and didn't lose until big-city school Terre Haute South stopped them in the Terre Haute Regional.

Tom Oliphant, his son Jeff, and the other Braves were 23-1 that year. L&M became a household word and Lyons and Marco were suddenly more than tiny dots on Indiana road maps. Bob Knight of Indiana University and other Division I coaches showed up to watch, their eyes on Jeff Oliphant and his buddy Patterson.

Fans by the hundreds came out of the woodwork and the cornfields and jumped on the L&M Express. Anyone who wanted a seat in the L&M gym had to arrive at the gym by 5:00 p.m. By the time the "B" team game started at 6:30, the gym was full.

When L&M met Washington Catholic in a battle of unbeatens late in the season, the game was moved to Switz City to accommodate a larger crowd. There were traffic jams for miles along each road leading to the gym. Tom Oliphant, who doubled as L&M athletic director, won't say how many thousands fans were at the game—"the fire marshal wouldn't appreciate it"—but the place was packed and people were sitting in the aisles and standing five or six deep behind the bleachers.

"Those two years I coached Jeff have been the greatest years of my life..."

L&M Coach Tom Oliphant   *Son, player Jeff Oliphant*

Chances are, even while the regional loss still stung, Oliphant and his band of upstarts started looking ahead to the 1984-85 season.

Oliphant, Patterson, Chad Grounds, and friends would spend the summer fine-tuning their game, knowing they no longer were an unknown, under-rated small-town team no one respected.

L&M was invited to play in the Hall of Fame Classic, a four-team showcase of some of the best teams in the state.The school was featured in a *Sports Illustrated* spread, was filmed by a crew from the National Basketball Hall of Fame, played before a statewide television network and was fabled in scores of newspaper stories.

It was heady stuff for teenage rural youths, but neither their hat nor chest sizes changed, nor their pursuit of more victories. The 1984-85 Braves lost one of the two Hall of Fame games, but didn't lose again until the semistate. When they cut down the nets at Terre Haute after winning the regional, it gave Tom Oliphant one of the greatest thrills of his life.

His greatest disappointment would come a week later. The fairy tale ended then when L&M lost in the championship game to Southridge. The book was closed on a fantastic 28-2 season.

It was a bitter pill, not only for the team, but the community. The pain would ease in time. L&M had proved small schools could still survive among the giants. Success would live in the newspaper clippings and as long as there were fans to repeat the stories to other fans.

Six weeks or so later in that spring of 1985, Jeff Oliphant and Tony Patterson were named by *The Indianapolis Star* to the Indiana All-Star team, an honor for a school with just thirty-five seniors.

Bob Knight's visits to L&M paid off. Jeff Oliphant entered IU that fall and, after a red-shirt year, finished his career there in the 1989-90 season and earned a degree in telecommunications.

The 6'6" Tony Patterson entered Purdue, but later transferred to South-ern Methodist where he also was a senior that season.

Tom Oliphant resigned as L&M coach after the 1988-89 season in order to watch Jeff play his last year at Indiana. He hasn't decided whether to return to coaching.

And L&M will soon become a part of White River High School, a new consolidation of Worthington, Switz City and L&M.

JEFF OLIPHANT, THE PLAYER: Jeff Oliphant always had a goal to shoot at from the time his dad put one in his bedroom. Each time the family moved, one of the first things father Tom did was to erect a backboard and goal.

The goal kept going up as Jeff grew older. He would play about every night, expecting his dad to rebound for him. "He was intent on playing basketball," his dad says.

He also was interested in football and baseball. He played football as a first grader at Dugger and his dad believes it made him a more aggressive basketball player. There was no football at Worthington when the family moved there, and Jeff spent his time at basketball on the third and fourth-grade teams. By the time he reached the sixth grade he was playing on the seventh-grade team. He played on both the seventh and eight-grade teams as a seventh grader.

He usually showed up at varsity practice, and as an eighth grader scrimmaged against varsity players. He was big enough even then to hold his own. He was a typical coach's son, a gym rat.

Coach Oliphant had no fear his son would get too much basketball. "Some kids get turned off if pushed too hard at times," Tom Oliphant agrees, "but I think the ones who really love the game want to work hard enough to learn the skills needed to play."

Jeff developed those skills by hours of practice. He learned about the game by being around it. He had listened to his father and grandfather talk about basketball from the time he was born. That gave him an advantage over other youngsters his age and it heightened his interest.

Tom Oliphant took his son on some scouting trips and Jeff picked up knowledge about the game by watching other players and observing other coaching strategies.

Coach Oliphant told Jeff, as well as his other players, that they would only get better by playing someone better than they were. "Play someone smarter and quicker than you are, go one-on-one against them in the summer and you'll be better the next season," he said.

That's why he sent Jeff to summer camps like Bob Knight's at Bloomington, the Five Star camp at Pittsburgh, and the B/C camp at Rensselaer.

By the time Jeff Oliphant reached junior high, his dad could see he could be a good player. On the floor, he had a sense of what would happen before it happened. That made him a better passer and gave him a lot of assists.

"You could tell at an early age that he understood the game and was aware of how it was to be played," his dad explains.

Some people disagreed with Tom Oliphant when he put his son on a weight program when he was six or seven. "His basket was probably six and a half foot off the ground and I bought him a little set of barbells with maybe ten pounds of weight on each side. Jeff would lift the weights, shoot, lift weights, shoot. I always made sure he shot the ball each time after he'd lifted the weights.

"I actually believe that gave him some strength in his arms so he could just go out on the floor and use his wrist to shoot. It gave him some extra range in his shooting," his dad said.

Fans who have watched Indiana University games the last four years know Jeff Oliphant is a good outside shooter. That may be the reason.

IN HIGH SCHOOL: Worthington, like L&M, was a small school and there was little doubt Jeff Oliphant was good enough for the varsity as a freshman. He missed the first game of the season with an injury, but he came off the bench in the second game and scored ten or twelve points to show that he deserved to play. He started the next game and all the games thereafter except when he was injured.

Most fans knew Jeff was good enough to play, and his dad heard few if any complaints for using him on the varsity.

As a sophomore, Jeff Oliphant helped lead Worthington to a 14-7 record. The team had some good shooters, and Coach Oliphant used his son as a point guard.

With Oliphant and some other players due to return, Worthington fans had high expectations for the season to follow. But that summer Tom Oliphant took the coaching job at L&M and he wasn't about to leave his son behind.

"It was a case," son Jeff says, "of Dad wanting to go back home where he had graduated."

Tom Oliphant admits some of the Worthington fans are still upset about the move, perhaps even a bit jealous. Others got over it and wished the Oliphants and L&M the best. A few told the coach it was the best move he could have made. "But I know for a fact the players were angry when we moved. They felt hurt by it and I can understand that. I had started Jeff with three juniors so four of the starters would have been back. The Worthington team didn't have as much success as expected so the feelings were pretty hard and bitter."

AT HOME: The Oliphants talked about the game at home when Jeff was in high school, but it was in junior high when the discussions were the most vocal.

"I wasn't his coach in junior high so I sat in the stands and watched him play. I was probably a little more critical when we got home and it would be pretty rough after a game if I thought he didn't play well.

"I might say 'you played pretty well tonight, Jeff, but here are some things you can work on.' I suppose maybe he got tired of hearing that and two or three times we got into arguments, leaving both of us mad. But we always got over it after a while."

Things got better at home when Jeff moved into high school.

Looking back, Tom Oliphant can analyze better how he handled son Jeff as a player:

"I may have put a little more pressure on Jeff in practices than I did other kids. I just expected him not to make mistakes and to do things right. That, on my part, wasn't right. Every kid is going to make mistakes. They are just sixteen, seventeen, and eighteen year olds."

Jeff Oliphant's main interest was basketball, but he was like any other teenager growing up in a rural area. He ran around with his friends, dated two or three different girls, and went fishing. At home, he kept to himself on weekday nights, studying or watching TV in his room.

"You might not see him for a couple of hours, then you'd hear the refrigerator door open and he'd be fixing himself a sandwich," his dad recalls.

MEMORIES: Tom Oliphant may or may not return to coaching, but, if he does, it will be hard to match those two years at L&M when Jeff played for him.

"Needless to say, those were the two best years that I was involved with in coaching. In fact, those two years have been the greatest years of my life. It was a great group of kids and Jeff and I were fortunate to have been associated with them."

TOO SOON IT'S OVER: Tom Oliphant watched son Tom and Tony Patterson play in the Indiana-Kentucky series and knew that things no longer would be the same.

He no longer would be the dominant influence on his son's life. Other coaches would be.

"When Jeff was a senior, Joby Wright, an Indiana University assistant coach, told me IU wanted Jeff as a player. I said, "When he gets there, he will be playing for Bob Knight, you and the other coaches. I'm now a father and a spectator."

Now Tom Oliphant can just sit back like any other father and watch his son play. The coaching belongs to Bob Knight.

"I might tell Jeff a thing or two once in a while, but he's twenty-one and he knows what he should be doing and shouldn't be doing," Tom Oliphant says.

THANKS TO DAD: Jeff Oliphant knows he can trace much of his success back to his dad.

"He always made things [connected with basketball] available to me. There was always some kind of hoop to shoot at and a ball to use. I learned a lot being around basketball from the time I started hanging around the gym in elementary school.

"He made sure I used the proper techniques. He always made me do things right."

Instead of working summers to earn money for college, Jeff Oliphant worked in the gym to become good enough to obtain a basketball scholarship. The work paid off. The scholarship came. Basketball remained a part of his life.

Digging Deep at Dugger

COACH JOE HART AND JOEY HART

It has been another long day for Joe Hart. He has taught art at Union-Dugger High School, coached the Bulldogs baseball team, and is ready to start the thirty-minute drive home to Bloomfield.

His son, Joey, however, wants to extend the day by working on his basketball in the gymnasium. He, too, has had a long day. He is a student at Union-Dugger and has played on his dad's baseball team. As a catcher, he should be tired. But basketball is his favorite sport, and Joey Hart, like most coaches' sons, is a gym rat.

Joe Hart relents and heads for the gym, too.

The progress Joey makes in the off-season will determine how much he progresses between his junior and senior years. The drive home can wait.

Joey Hart is at Union-Dugger by design. His dad brought him into the school system as a seventh grader for two reasons: Joey appeared to be a good prospect, and Joe Hart wanted the privilege of coaching him.

Guy Glover, the athletic director at Bloomfield, had coached his son in high school. He told Joe Hart it would be an experience he should never pass up.

SHOP TALK: If they choose, Joe and Joey Hart can talk about a lot of things on the drive home and on the way to school the next day. If the talk is basketball, they can think back to the time Joey was still in his crib, a rubber ball at his side. And the time he first was old enough to hold it.

Or, they can move ahead in time and remember the twenty-by-twenty-foot outdoor basketball court at the house where they lived. They can remember the regulation goal and the small one Joe Hart put up for his son. It was there Joey, at age three or four, learned to shoot a basketball. And they can remember Joey keeping statistics at games when he was in the second grade.

Joe Hart waited until Joey was in the fifth grade to start teaching him

techniques. That was the year Joey had the thrill of seeing his dad's team win the Greene County tournament. It was Joe Hart's first year as varsity coach and his team was just 1-4 at the time. The Bulldogs won the first two games, one in overtime, the other by a point. That set up the championship game with Eastern, the favorite. Hart's team pulled off the upset.

That night, the captain of that team took young Joey Hart upstairs and tucked in the youngster who even then looked ahead to the time he could cut another net from a goal.

In the years to come, Joey Hart would spend hours on hours in gymnasiums. He played with his friends at Bloomfield and on occasions Guy Glover would let him in the gym.

Joey Hart played guard in grade school because he wasn't very big. That would turn out to be a bonus when he grew to 6'4" and could still handle the ball well, shoot from the perimeter, and play inside or outside.

Coach Hart and player Hart can look back to Joey's play in junior high and as a freshman. There were hints he could develop into a good player.

Joey Hart confesses he wasn't the greatest eighth-grade player. That was when his pursuit of perfection began. He had realized it would take work and dedication to become better than average.

He was on the junior varsity as a freshman. And he still recalls how badly he wanted a varsity jersey although no one else thought he deserved one. He went to every varsity practice, which meant he went through two workouts a day. He may have reminded his dad, on the drive home, that the other guard on the "B" team was given a varsity uniform "and I didn't get one."

It was then that Joey Hart realized he would receive no special treatment even though he was the coach's son.

Joe Hart was no different than other coaches. He knew if he used Joey fans would say it was favoritism. But he also knew that Joey should be treated as fairly as any other player.

Joey moved up to the varsity as a sophomore, a difficult transition, possibly because he was putting too much pressure on himself. He averaged four points a game over the first nine games and was reluctant to shoot after missing a shot.

Coach Hart worked with him over the Christmas break, and the change was dramatic. Over the last nine games, Joey averaged 15 points and his shooting percentage improved about twenty percent.

Joe Hart looks back and says the game that turned Joey around came against Linton, which had won the Greene County Tourney. Joey was 7-for-7 from the field and 5-for-5 from the free-throw line in that game.

Although Joey improved, the team still had its problems. The chemistry

needed to mold a team wasn't there. "The group just didn't play well together," the elder Hart says. "I think there was some animosity. We had quite
a few seniors that year and I think that's going to happen, especially if a
younger player is moved into the lineup. I don't think it would have mattered
if it had been Joey or somebody else."

Joey Hart senses that some of the older players resented the fact he was
playing, that he was the son of the coach. And to make matters more compli-
cated, he was separated from the classmates he had played with earlier.

Some fans criticized both Joe and Joey Hart early in the season. "I didn't
mind them getting on me because I've had that before. But when they get on
your son, no matter if you are a coach or not, it still hurts. It bothered me
and I think it bothered him some, too."

That criticism faded later in the season when Joey Hart started playing
better. The team finished 7 and 17, but went to the final game of the sectional.
He was on the Terre Haute all-sectional team, which indicates how much he
improved during the season.

THE TURNAROUND: Joey Hart's experience as a junior (1988-89)
was a complete turnaround from his sophomore season. He was with players
he had worked with earlier, the chemistry was a good mix, and the team
finished the season with a 22-3 mark.

Joey had averaged 9.7 points a game as a sophomore. As a junior, he
took only 11 shots a game but averaged 18.7 points for a .567 shooting
percentage, had 125 assists and 89 steals, and seldom heard a discouraging
word from fans.

He made all-county, all-sectional, and all-regional teams, two conference first teams and was the most valuable player in the Greene County
tourney. And as he had done in the fifth grade, he watched his dad cut down
nets, this time after winning the Greene County tournament and the Clay City
sectional. This time Joey was on the team, reliving a dream he had kept alive
for six years.

There was no resentment against Joey Hart. "The seniors were really
good to me," Joey Hart recalls. "In a way it was like our team was a family.
We weren't all really close, but we got along really well and if anybody had
a problem we helped each other."

ENCOURAGING WORDS: What advice would Joe Hart give to a
parent who is not a coach, but wants his son to be a basketball player?

"Kids have to be taught that basketball takes a lot of hard work. We
have so many kids who don't work at the game at home. A lot of your good
players are made at home."

Joey Hart spends an awful lot of time working at home, shooting at two
baskets, one for three-point shots—on the garage—and one on a post.

Coach Hart says parents need to rebound for their sons (and daughters) and get them interested. But he warned that too many parents want their kids to play a lot more than the kids do. "That's a bad situation for the coach, for the player, and for the parent. All three of them will be disappointed."

Joe Hart has been fortunate. Joey, he says, "just seems to want to keep going. People say he's going to get burned out, but I see no evidence of that. I can truthfully say I have never had to make him play. He wants to go to camp, he wants to play in summer leagues, he just wants to play."

Joey Hart agrees. "I get up in the morning in the summer and shoot thirty-five to forty minutes. I need to build myself up [during the summer of 1989] so I can be physically strong enough to play in college.

He says he spends four to five hours a day during the summer improving his game and strengthening his body.

FATHER AND SON: Coach Joe Hart says, "I'm sure that I'm harder on him than the other kids. A lot of times I take out things on him when I get mad at the team."

That means some of those thirty-minute drives home may not be too comfortable for Joey Hart.

But Joey sees it differently: "Dad usually is not real hard on me right after a game. He'll tell me some things that I can work on that next Monday. He's pretty good about what I did wrong in practice or in a game."

SATISFACTION: Joe Hart's greatest satisfaction is seeing how Joey has developed and improved. "His attitude and work ethics have been great," he said, looking ahead to Joey's senior season in 1989-90, when he returned with one other starter from the 1988-89 team that went to the final game of the regional before losing to Terre Haute South.

AT HOME: Unlike some coaches, Joe Hart admits basketball is one of the prime subjects for conversations at home.

"It's not so much our games. We talk about the other teams in our area and about other players, the NBA and college basketball. Joey is a big New York Mets baseball fan, but basketball is the big item."

Sons of some coaches spend the summer playing basketball rather than working at jobs. Joe Hart says it is that way at the Hart residence. "We've got a yard that takes about three hours to mow and we [he and Joey] have agreed to split the time. I gripe sometimes when I'm going up the hill on the mower and look down and see him shooting baskets. But, I get to thinking that it may pay off when the weather is cold in January and it makes mowing in the heat easier."

Joe Hart does put his son to work at times. They line and paint emblems on gym floors in southern Indiana during the summer months.

DIVERSIONS: Lest anyone think Joey Hart's life is all basketball, it should be pointed out that he ranks fourth in a 1990 class of 40 students. He scored 1030 on the SAT. He likes to fish. He has a girlfriend at Dugger, which means his dates are also thirty minutes away.

THE FUTURE: Both coach and player looked forward to the 1989-90 season. Coach Hart knew that would be his son's last year, that after that he no longer would be his coach.

Joey Hart expected to be back in the Terre Haute sectional. "I'd give my eye teeth to beat the Terre Haute team in a big upset."

It was a dream they'd probably talk about, too, on that long drive from Bloomfield to Dugger and back again.

Oh, Say, He Can Play!

COACH HERSCHELL ALLEN AND SON MICHAEL ALLEN

Coach Herschell Allen's Shakamak team was struggling late in the 1986-87 season when he decided it was time to elevate his son, Michael, to the varsity.

The payoff came immediately. Shakamak had won but two games when he inserted Michael and Brian Rehmel, who had also played on the "B" team. They started against Eminence. Michael Allen was a freshman, and the Eminence coach figured the pressure might be too much for him.

The coach kept yelling, "Foul No. 10! Foul No. 10! Foul No. 10."

Herschell Allen was licking his chops. No. 10 was his son. And he knew No. 10 would put the ball in the basket.

And he did! Michael Allen hit ten straight free throws and Shakamak won the game. Anyone who thought Michael Allen had moved into the lineup because he was the coach's son could forget it. The kid knew how to play the game.

When Michael made those free throws, it took a lot of pressure off himself and his dad. And it helped when the team won two of its last four games and set the stage for even better things to come.

One of the highlights came the following season (1987-88) when Michael Allen and Brian Rehmel led Shakamak to its first sectional championship in 22 years and then upset highly-ranked Terre Haute South in the regional. Rehmel had a career-high 30 points. Herschell Allen's decision a year earlier had paid off.

OH, SAY, HE COULD PLAY: Basketball seemed to come naturally for Michael Allen. He was around the game almost from the time he was born, toddling around the gym as soon as he could walk.

By the time he was three or four he was replaying the game when he returned home. He started with the National Anthem, hand over heart. He had his own uniform, imitated the players and learned to flash the No. 1 sign common to all players.

He jumped off a desk and dunked the ball in an imaginary goal on the wall.

Herschell Allen taught his son how to hold the ball, how to put his hand in the proper position, and to make sure he did things correctly.

"I didn't let him, or my younger son, Mark, shoot at ten-foot goals when they were young. I had them shoot at a level they could reach and demanded that they use the correct form. Too many kids develop bad habits that are difficult to correct later."

Michael started playing organized basketball as a fifth grader. By then he had advanced past other kids in his class, could dribble or shoot layups with either hand.

Michael Allen went scouting with his father and soon was giving his dad advice about players to watch. He observed the better players and adapted what they did. He picked up things quickly, his dad said. "Being around the game as the son of a coach was a big plus for him."

As he grew older, Michael spent more and more time in the gym, seldom missing a day even when he was involved in spring sports. Michael, a shortstop, also has his dad as his baseball coach.

But basketball is his sport and Coach Allen could tell fairly early he could be an outstanding player. "He got his shooting fundamentals down and was interested in the game."

Michael Allen played on teams in the fifth, sixth, seventh and eighth grades that seldom lost—a total of four games in four years. He was a big scorer in those games, but as he grew older he learned to do more than just shoot.

By the time he was a junior in the 1988-89 season, he was a complete player. He had averaged 18.6 points a game playing off guard as a sophomore. His statistics were even better as a junior, when his dad moved him to point guard "out of necessity."

That season (1988-89) he averaged 24.6 points a game, but still had 4.9 assists a game and was the second leading rebounder although he played in the backcourt and was only six feet tall.

BEFORE AND AFTER:
Budding jock Michael Allen
(left), and more recently in full
stride as a guard at Shakamak,
where he's coached by his
dad, Herschell

Whether it is basketball or baseball, Michael Allen works to improve his game. When he went 0 for 4 in a baseball game, he stepped into the batting cage later in the day in an attempt to improve his swing.

"I don't have to get on him. He wants to be good, which is what it takes to succeed in sports," his dad adds.

Michael Allen has picked up a lot from Steve Alford's workout videotape. Almost daily, he works on his ball-handling, makes sure he shoots 100 jump-shots and 100 free throws, lifts weights, and tries to build up his body. He observes that regimen religiously.

THE MOST IMPORTANT THINGS: Much of Michael Allen's life has centered around basketball, but his parents have taught him to keep things in perspective.

"We spell it out," his father says. "The first thing in life is to be faithful to God. The second thing is his family and the third thing is school. After that comes athletics, then cars and girls and other things."

Coach Allen adds, "As long as you keep those things in order then you're going to be in good shape. We talk about those things in our chapter of the Fellowship of Christian Athletes and we constantly remind Michael of them at home."

Michael has done well in keeping his priorities in order, but could have done better in the classroom, according to his dad's assessment.

"He's a good Christian kid, who respects his parents. He has a girlfriend, who accepts the fact that basketball comes first."

PRESSURE: Michael Allen faced little criticism for being the coach's son. "In a small school you know everyone. So it hasn't been the problem it might be in a larger school," he explains. But he admits he felt some pressure, or at least apprehension, at the start of his freshman year.

"I really didn't know what to expect and I figured there might be some complaints if I did get to play right off the bat. But it wasn't as much as I figured there would be. The people in town didn't appear to expect any more out of me than any other player."

He had practiced with the upperclassmen as an eighth grader and was accepted by the team, which made the transition from junior high to varsity easier.

AT HOME: The Allens don't concentrate on basketball all the time. Coach Allen doesn't think it is healthy. "We try to leave it on the floor as much as possible. I try never to use Michael as an example if things go wrong at practice or in a game.

"Michael almost always gives 110%. And he knows what I want," his dad explains. "If we have a bad practice, he knows what we have to do to correct those situations."

Coach Allen does spend some time at home showing Michael what he wants done on the floor. And after games, the Allens sometimes go home and verbally replay the game over a pizza. If Coach Allen has brought home a tape, the family may watch the game again, especially if it was a pleasurable one.

LOOKING AHEAD: Herschell Allen doesn't expect to be coaching when his younger son, Mark, reaches high school. He won't push him to play athletics: "If he doesn't want to play, I'm not the type who will make him. If he wants to play, I'm going to help him as much as I can. I see so many people, even here in our community, who really don't take the time to be with their kids.

"I take that very, very seriously and I'm going to make sure I spend time with Mark when Michael moves on to college and starts playing for someone else."

Michael would like someday to play in the National Basketball Association, a goal he knows only a few players attain. And eventually he wants to work in physical education or some form of recreation so he can help youngsters.

And he doesn't rule out being a coach. If so, he would like to coach his own son. His experience with his father has been a pleasant one. He's learned "fun" starts with fundamentals—and endures if you've got the right priorities.

In His Father's Footsteps

PHIL BUCK AND SONS LARRY AND JOE BUCK

Bobby Wilkerson, Ray Tolbert, Winston Morgan, Stew Robinson, Larry Buck, Joe Buck! Six players, one coach—Phil Buck, a man of candor and deep-rooted belief in the virtues of hard work.

Wilkerson, Tolbert, Morgan, and Robinson played for Phil Buck at Madison Heights before performing at Indiana University for Bob Knight.

Larry and Joe Buck were Phil's sons—he was their coach, their father, and their mentor.

For an insight into what these six players and hundreds of others have learned from Phil Buck, let's turn back the calendar to 1951. Harry Truman was president, television was in its infancy, Americans were fighting in Korea, and young men looking for coaching jobs were finding them in small towns that still had their own high schools.

Fresh out of Indiana University where he had played for Branch Mc-Cracken, Phil Buck picked Flora High School as a place to start his career. A year later Uncle Sam needed Buck more than Flora did, and he served with the U.S. Army for two years.

Discharged, Buck stopped at IU for a year as an assistant coach, then returned home to Rossville to coach high school. He was at Rossville six years, nearby Frankfort for five, then moved to Madison Heights in 1967.

Phil Buck's 1988-89 season at Rossville was his thirty-fifth as a high school head coach. Add up the victories, count the losses, and you get 480-338. Only five active coaches had more victories at the end of that season.

Phil Buck is proud of the young men he's sent to play at IU, but he's just as proud of the scores of other players he has coached and who turned out to be solid citizens.

And, chances are, deep down, he's prouder still of his sons Larry and Joe. Larry, his first son, graduated in 1973, attended General Motors Institute, and now works at a GM plant in Albany, Georgia. Joe is head basketball coach and assistant principal at Lapel High School and has to match wits with his dad when their teams meet each year.

Phil Buck is as Hoosier as persimmons, pawpaws, pumpkins, and basketball, and as down-to-earth as a farmer plowing the fields back in Clinton County where he grew up. It is no wonder that people listen when he talks basketball. And when he talks, it's experience and common-sense analysis they hear.

Chances are nobody would have been a better coach for his sons than Phil Buck himself. And both will say they are better men because of him. Yet, it's something he wouldn't want to do again.

He thinks it hamstrung Larry and Joe too much. The public, and sometimes other players and students, he says, are awfully hard on a coach's son. Like a minister's son, a coach's son is expected to be better than normal.

"As a coach I was harder on my two sons than I was on anyone else. As I look back I would not want to go through it again. I don't think it was fair to the boys. But at the same time, I don't think Larry or Joe ever were criticized by the fans or the student body. I think most of the time they felt sorry for them."

After practice one day, an outspoken little fellow came up to Coach Buck, looked up, and asked, "Coach, do you mind if I say something?" Buck replied, "No, go ahead." All the player said was, "Thank God I'm not your son." The coach believes most teammates felt both Larry and Joe had earned the right to play and that their father/coach picked on them too much.

"I would have preferred, if it could have been done, [to send] Joe and

Larry to Anderson High School to play for Ray Estes [then the Anderson coach]. Knowing they might have beat me, I still think it would have been fairer to those two boys had they got to do that."

Perhaps Phil Buck is being harder on himself than he was on his sons. Joe Buck, fourteen years after the experience, doesn't see it that way. Looking back, he says, "I would definitely want to play for my father. I believe 'Coach' is someone whom you should believe in and respect. I can't think of anyone that I trust or respect more than my father."

Phil Buck has this advice for coaches who have their sons as players: "When you walk into the gym you have to look at your son as just another one of your players. You have to relay that to the other squad members, but you just can't walk out and tell them.

"You do it by your actions, the way you coach, the way you handle your child. The other players have to know that you look at your son just like you look at them."

That, he insists, is hard to do.

A youngster playing for his father can also learn from Coach Buck: "Remember that your father is a basketball coach. And he has to put a squad

GOOD LUCK: Larry Buck (left) with brother Joe before a Lapel game

together than can win. He can't be thinking about whether you are his son or not. He is going to treat you like he does the other kids. Don't take it personal. You should expect the same thing out of him as you do the other kids on the team, nothing more, nothing less."

AT HOME: When Phil Buck walks into the gym, it is all basketball. Once he leaves, it is just the opposite. Basketball is over for the day. Basketball, he insists, has never been discussed at home, either when his sons were home or after they left.

"That may sound unbelievable," he says, "but we did not talk about it. If something happened here in the gym that was unpleasant, I never mentioned it at home.

"We talked about fishing, what lake we were going to in the summer, and that type of thing. But we didn't talk about basketball.

"To this day, Norma Jean and I do not discuss basketball at home. It is not a thing that is done by design. I am just not interested in talking basketball with my family and the family is really not interested, either."

Both Larry and Joe Buck were honor-roll students and their mother insisted they do their homework before they watched any television. And, unlike many families today, the Bucks dined together at supper, regardless of the time.

"We were raised in the old-type homes and Mrs. Buck always waited until the entire family was together to serve the meal."

Mrs. Buck did play an important part in making things easier between Coach Buck and his two sons. Like other players, the Buck boys sometimes thought the coach was an old fogey who didn't understand young people; they didn't understand why he did some things he did. Sometimes they thought he was too hard on them. That's when their mother listened.

"If it hadn't been for her, things could have been more difficult," Phil Buck admits.

Occasionally teachers said something when they thought he was being too tough on Joe or Larry. When that happened, Coach Buck tried to "do some things to relieve that pressure."

LARRY AND JOE AS PLAYERS: Phil Buck never told his sons they had to go to the gym or that they had to play the game: "I always left it up to them whether they wanted to be here [at the gym].

"It's like kids in our summer program. I never tell a kid he has to be here. I tell him the gym is open, that it's a recreational program, that we'd like to have him. That's when you find out whether a kid wants to play. If he has enough desire and initiative, he'll be here."

For Larry and Joe, being at the gym was fun and they wanted to be there. But as youngsters, they didn't have the run of the gym, and except for one short trip they weren't allowed to ride on the team bus. They were never team mascots or towel boys and they seldom went with their dad when he scouted other teams unless the entire family went along.

Phil Buck explains why: "I always left Norma Jean and them out of it. I never exposed them to the public. I think that sometimes when you do that you are criticized for it. And you have a lot of people in the stands who have boys the same age as your son who would love to be able to do the same thing."

Buck's sons had an outside goal in front of their home where they learned some of the basics of the game. He told them things they would have to be able to do to become players. And, to prove he wanted them to learn the game, he might reward them for certain things . . . "like hitting a certain number of free-throws out of fifty attempts."

Larry and Joe picked up a lot by being around older players. And Phil Buck admits he was fortunate to have players in high school they could emulate.

Junior-high kids are hero-worshippers, he explains. "I think it is awfully important that the high school athletes create good images. By being around the locker room and around the game, they learned about athletics and they learned different philosophies of life. They were around different kinds of people at an early age."

The Buck boys started playing organized ball at Roosevelt elementary school in Anderson. Joe's fifth-grade team won the city championship.

They also played junior-high basketball, but Phil Buck encouraged them to play other sports and each also played football and ran track.

Here, again, it's Phil Buck's philosophy: "Norma Jean and I both felt that organized sports were awfully important, but not for the same reason some people think. Not for scholarships, not for monetary reasons, but for the fact it is important for a young boy to be involved with school activities where they have certain requirements, certain standards to meet.

"I've been asked often what is the most important time in a young man's life. I say from three to five, and people think I mean that age range. I say no. From three to five in the afternoon. That's when kids get in trouble. That's when kids leave school. They are full of zip and pizzazz. They've been tied down all day and if they don't have some parental guidance or some kind of school activity they are going to get rid of that energy in some way. And often it is in the wrong way."

Larry Buck is two years older than Joe. He was a perfectionist who found it more difficult to play for his dad than Joe did. Larry was a junior, the sixth man, when Phil Buck's Madison Heights team lost to Gary West in the afternoon game of the state finals.

His dad says Larry "thought he had to be perfect to play. He really was an excellent shooter, but it worried him so much when he missed a shot it did affect his play."

Larry Buck came along at a time when Madison Heights had some excellent basketball players. Larry was a small forward, 6'2", so he played the sixth-man role as a senior, the same year Joe moved into the starting lineup as a sophomore.

"We didn't have a point guard. No one to run the ball club," Coach Buck explains. "We saw this after the season started and we moved Joe up to fill that role."

That was a difficult season, for the coach, for Larry, and for Joe. It was the first time in three years the school didn't win the always-tough Anderson sectional.

The coach may have criticized Joe more than he did Larry. "Larry was so conscientious, his problem was that he couldn't relax. Joe was the opposite. He was the more daring, the more challenging to his dad. So I was constantly on him to give it 100 percent. If your own son doesn't do it, there isn't anyone on the squad who is going to do it."

Friends sometimes advised Phil Buck to play Larry more. "He was an excellent outside shooter and he was an intelligent player, but he didn't have the speed some other kids had. So I thought he should have all those things before I could move him in front of other players. I thought that would be harder on him."

If Phil Buck's sons did something wrong in games or practices, they were criticized just like any other players. "There were no exceptions made. When I look back to the time I took them out of the game to make constructive criticism, I never thought of them as my sons.

"I took them out of a game as players, young men who had make great plays and contributions or as players who had done nothing. It was made known to them right then what they had done right or wrong."

Joe Buck graduated from high school in 1975 after being on the team that went to the semistate. The years since have given Phil Buck a time to reflect on his role as the boys' coach.

"We have become a lot closer since they played for me. We laugh about things that happened in practice and they tell me some of the things that went on I might not have known about at the time."

In the end, he says, "it all worked out great."

'IT'S STILL FUN': Thirty-five years haven't dulled Phil Buck's enthusiasm for the game.

"It's fun. I have fun taking a different group of kids every year and attempting to mold them into a working unit that can win. And no one has a tougher schedule than ours. It's tough to win with that schedule even if we have a good bunch of kids.

"We have just one junior high feeding in here. So we follow those seventh and eighth-grade kids and see how they progress. Then we have them in our freshman program and by the time we get them as sophomores, juniors, and seniors they are almost like our own sons.

"To me it is just fun to watch them progress. Some kids you don't think will make it develop a lot of heart and play. Some who have a tremendous amount of athletic ability in the seventh grade may not have the heart for the game or don't like the competition and they don't progress.

"Every day is different. I have not had a boring day in thirty-five years. There have never been two days the same. I don't believe I have ever had two days out of those thirty-five where the problems have been the same."

And he adds, "I still feel like I am effective as a basketball coach. And as long as I feel that way, I'd like to stay in it."

JOE BUCK, PLAYER, COACH: Joe Buck didn't step into a head coaching job just because his dad was a successful coach. He went to Lapel after graduating from Purdue and was junior-high coach for four years before being assistant coach under Dallas Hunter for four years.

He took over as head coach in the 1988-89 season. He doubles as assistant principal at the 375-student school.

His second game as Lapel coach was against his dad's Madison Heights team. "That was an exciting time," Joe Buck recalls: "There was a lot of publicity about a son coaching against his father. It was something I always wanted to do. The game didn't turn out like I would have hoped, and he beat us handily." The score was 87-55.

There will be more encounters between father and son. And each will give Joe Buck a chance to think back to the time he played for his father.

Joe Buck recalls being a sophomore starter was very hard. It was a year in which the team had a rare losing season. A lot of talent graduated from the squad that had gone to the state finals in 1972, but the expectation of fans was still high.

"There was a lot of pressure, a lot of hard times. If you are losing and the coach's son is playing, especially at a young age, there is going to be a lot more criticism."

Joe Buck didn't get much criticism, but what he did hear bothered him. Another thing that bothered him was that he was playing more than his big brother, Larry, who was a senior.

"Now that I look back," Buck added, "I think that put a lot of hardships on my family—my father, my mother, and my brother. I think they protected me. They didn't want me to feel bad about it and they were very very supportive."

To Larry's credit, Joe Buck says, "he was very positive, very supportive. He always encouraged me to do my best."

Joe Buck realized his dad put more pressure on him than on other players. "I had a lot of people tell me they didn't know how I could handle some of the pressure I went through. I realized what Dad was doing. He didn't want anybody to ever say he was giving me an easy road.

"But he was always fair."

Growing up in a coach's family, Joe Buck knew the pressure involved. "When I was a little boy, it really, really bothered me when my dad's team lost . . .and it still does today."

No one was happier than senior Joe Buck when the 1974-75 Madison Heights team was highly successful. The team was ranked in the top ten most

Anderson Herald-Bulletin

LIVING LEGENDS: Madison Heights Coach Phil Buck shares a moment with Anderson's Norm Held

of the season and won the Anderson sectional and regional before losing to Fort Wayne North in the semistate.

"A lot of the pressure was off, it was my last year, the year I stepped forward as the team leader and could do a lot of things for my father. I could lead behind the scenes because I knew what he wanted to get out of the team. And I was able to help him do that."

The Bucks seldom talked basketball at home then, but now the situation is almost reversed. Now Joe and his father almost always talk basketball when they are together. "The things I have learned, and am continuing to learn from Dad, are definite advantages," says Joe Buck.

Now a coach, Joe Buck also has a clearer perspective on how a father should coach a son:

"You have to treat your son as close to equal as you have any other player you have ever coached. If you show favoritism to him you are going to make his life miserable. At the same time, you cannot be extremely difficult on him.

"You can't do what the fans expect you to do or what the student body would like you to do. You must do what you think is right, the things you have always done as a coach."

He has this advice for the son:

"You can't let allegations that you are being shown favoritism bother you. You have to go about your game and think about what you want to get out of it."

Would he now want to coach his own son?

"I have often thought about that. Right now I have two girls and I don't have to face that question. But I think any coach, down deep, would like the opportunity to coach his son. If we have a boy, I would want to coach him.

"If I had my career to live over, I would want to play for my father. I wouldn't pick another situation. So I think I would enjoy coaching my son."

A LETTER FROM JOE: Joe Buck was home from college when he attended a game in which the son of a coach was booed. The team wasn't having a successful season, and the coach's son was an easy target. Showing unusual maturity for a college student, Joe sat down and wrote the lad a letter in which he said:

"You have to understand the type of fans who attend basketball games. They want to win and that is all some of them consider. Consider the source. Take pride in yourself and your father, the coach. Continue to do the things your father tells you to do. Don't change anything that you've been told to do to become a great basketball player, and things will work out for you."

He relates things did work out for that player, the team was successful, and the same people who had been booing the son and criticizing the coach for playing his son later said, "This kid is great. I'm glad he is playing for our team."

AN ANECDOTE: Joe Buck remembers sitting on the bench as a sophomore after Madison Heights had just lost an important game.

"We hadn't played very well. Dad started at the end of the bench and I was on the opposite end. He worked his way down the row. He told each player what he didn't appreciate about them in the game and pointed out the things they would have to change. I sat waiting. The closer he got, the more nervous I got. He finally worked his way down to me. I expected the worst. But once again, he was firm, but fair."

And that, after all, may be the greatest thing a son can expect from his father.

Accentuate the Positive

COACH NORM HELD AND SON DAVID HELD

SCENARIO: The clock is running down in a 1979 regional basketball game between Carmel and Anderson.

Carmel, which had blitzed the Indians a month earlier, is leading by a point. With three seconds to play, David Held gets the ball at the top of the key and fires a jump shot from 17 feet.

The shot is good. Anderson wins by a point. The coach's son is a hero. The team advances to the championship game of the state finals before losing to Muncie Central.

SCENARIO: It is a year later. Anderson is at home to meet rival Muncie Central.

David Held, the hero of the Carmel game, is having a bad night. Nothing he does seems to work out right. The fans, long on expectations, short on memory, begin to boo, boos that can be heard down on the bench by Coach Norm Held, if not out on the floor by his son David.

* * *

Two games, two different emotions, proof that basketball mirrors life. Bad times follow good times, good days follow bad.

Coach Norm Held has seen more good days than bad. Starting the

1989-90 season, he had sent his teams into battle 719 times and seen them win 502 games for a .698 victory percentage. He had taken teams to the state finals four times, always in search of that elusive dream, the brass ring, always within reach, but almost untouchable.

The pursuit of victories goes on. Norm Held, better than most, knows why. It's the same thing that may keep businessmen and political leaders involved in their pursuits. But Norm Held isn't afraid to admit why he stays with it.

"There is an element of ego that's involved. When you get down to realistic facts, it because you've been in a position where the people of the community identify with you as the basketball coach.

"If you walk away from that, you give up that identity. Maybe that's it. But I still enjoy teaching basketball. I still enjoy being around the players. It helps keep you young. And it's still a challenge. The challenge will never go away."

Norm Held has exposed forty-eight players to the excitement of the Final Four and had four seniors named to Indiana all-star teams, including co-Mr. Basketball Troy Lewis (1984). He coached John Harter, the 1983 winner of the Trester Award, the highest individual honor available to a player in the Indiana state tournament.

And he had an Academic All-State player in his son, David Held.

And he had another son, Don, who decided not to compete for a spot on his dad's team.

ONE WHO PLAYED: In the beginning, Norm Held was like most other fathers. He wanted his older son David to be an outstanding basketball player and an outstanding athlete.

But, as a coach, he knew that was not very realistic. He knew he could expose David to the game and hope he would like it. But he knew if David wasn't very quick, or very tall, or very strong there would be obstacles to overcome.

But his son did overcome those hurdles. Young David started coming to the gym as a youngster. To be with his father, he ran from the elementary school in Danville, Illinois, to the high school gym there.

By being around basketball he absorbed it, osmosis-like, gaining knowledge which would help offset his physical limitations. He liked basketball and his fundamentals were excellent. But Coach Held knew he would have to learn to get off shots quickly and to cheat on quickness if he was going to be able to play.

When Held moved to Anderson, son David found a spot on an eighth-grade team of good athletes. He became a leader of that group and his dad noted the progress he made. David played with the same unit as a freshman and sophomore and moved onto the varsity as a junior.

The highlight of his career came when he hit the shot that defeated Carmel and sent Anderson enroute to the semistate and on to the finals in Indianapolis.

The next year, David Held and the four players he was with as freshmen and sophomores were seniors, a small but cohesive unit with the right chemistry that resulted in a successful regular season.

But the Indians were playing Muncie Central in the Wigwam when fans proved they could be cruel. David Held wasn't having a good game, his dad admits, adding, "I don't know what was wrong with him."

Some of the fans didn't care about past victories. They turned their venom on David Held and their boos could be heard all the way to the Anderson bench, perhaps out onto the floor.

Norm Held acknowledges, "Anderson fans have been very, very loyal. They've been very good to me. But in that particular instance they were a little brutal. They forgot the good things David had done even though he wasn't playing well that night. They had a legitimate complaint."

Held took his son out of the game, then let him return. "He played a little better but he struggled," Coach Held adds. It may have been the only bad game he had at Anderson."

David Held always said he didn't hear the boos, but his dad did and he thinks maybe David did, too. Norm Held hasn't forgotten. "When I heard

"He was a good, solid role player who got the ball to the right people."
—Coach Norm Held
on his son, David

the boos, I just happened to look up into the crowd, which I seldom do, and I saw my younger boy [Don] walk out of the gym. And I knew why he was leaving.

"And then I took a glance at his mother and I saw the anguish on her face and of course as the coach and father it bothered me."

That 1979-80 season came to an abrupt end when Anderson lost the sectional finale on a last-second shot to Highland, 76-75.

David Held finished the season with averages of 10 points and 10 assists per game (a school record). He became the first Anderson player to be named to the Academic All-State team.

Going into the 1989-90 season, he still held the single-season assist record, the single-game assist record and two free-throw records.

"That," his dad adds, "is not to say he should have been an Indiana All-Star, because he shouldn't. He wasn't that kind of a player. He was just a good, solid role player and a very good leader who got the ball to the right people."

Two members of that team, Shawn Teague and Henry Johnson, were named to the 1980 Indiana All-Star team.

David Held played basketball at Augusta College in Augusta, Georgia, graduated and, his dad boasts, was one of the few people who passed, on the first attempt, all four parts of the exam to be a certified public accountant. David Held now lives in San Diego.

THE BOY IN THE BLEACHERS: When Norm Held's younger son, Don, decided to drop basketball, it took a lot of pressure off his dad. Norm Held explains why:

"He could shoot well and do some other things. But we didn't have the right set of circumstances that we had with David. He just didn't fit into the program and he knew it. So he didn't come out for the team as a junior.

"I've always appreciated that because I don't know what I would have done. I probably would never have cut him. I probably would have kept him on the team.

"But he always would have felt like he had taken the place of somebody who maybe should have been there. I felt that was a good sign of a quality kid."

Instead of basketball, Don Held played baseball, winning the Carl Erskine Award given to the outstanding player on the Anderson High School baseball team.

Don Held went to Indiana University and now is a financial consultant in San Diego.

LEADERSHIP: Coaches' sons turn out to be leaders on the basketball floor more often than not. Norm Held thinks that may come naturally.

"They are around the game so much they know it better than other players. Other kids identify with them, accept them as leaders because their dads are the coaches.

"In David's case, they knew if they did what they were supposed to do, he would get the ball to them. They liked that."

COACH AND PLAYER, FATHER AND SON: It's hard work, Norm Held stresses, for a coach to separate the father-son, player-coach roles.

"It was difficult to set David aside and not think of him constantly as my son. But, I don't think I ever did anything for him as a player that I wouldn't do for any of the other players.

"I never took the game home with me or gave David any kind of harassment at home over basketball. At home, we stressed the academic part of school."

At the gym, Norm Held admits he was harder on his son than on other players. "There is no question about it."

Norm Held gives himself good grades for being able to separate the player from the son, with this exception:

"The only time I ever touched a kid or grabbed a kid was when I grabbed his shirt. It is something I'll never forget. I was totally embarrassed by it, probably the most embarrassing moment I have had in basketball. I'm sure that it looked a lot worse to fans than it was.

"I apologized to him. At practice and in games, I always thought of him as another player. But I grabbed him as my son. It would never have entered my mind to do that to another player."

Norm Held said that incident may have turned around some fans who hadn't been on David's side before.

A COACH'S EXPERIENCE SPEAKS: With two sons and twenty-eight years as a coach, Norm Held has some advice for coaches who may have their sons as players. Make sure, he says, to separate the son and the player, even though it is hard to do. Don't expect your son to be more than he can be, and don't set your goals so high that he doesn't have any chance to fulfill your dreams.

And make sure that you don't mistreat him because that's easy to do. In practice, don't make an example of your son.

When Norm Held got on David about basketball, he did it at the gym in front of the other players. "Sometimes I was too hard on him and I think most coaches subconsciously are harder on their sons. But fortunately he was the kind of kid who could handle it and it worked in his favor because the other kids came to his defense if I got obnoxious about it."

For sons of coaches, Held offers this: "Be able to handle criticism, because Daddy sees in you what he wanted to see, or did see, in himself. He wants you to be his superstar and that may be beyond your capabilities. Do the best you can. That's all you can do."

HE'D DO IT AGAIN: Looking back a decade later, Norm Held, would you want to coach your son again?

"Yes, I would."

Two-Letter Men

COACH JOE NULL AND SONS DAVID AND SAM

Joe Null never made any special effort to encourage his sons to be basketball players. He was too busy when they were young.

He was married shortly after graduating from Terre Haute Gerstmeyer and had two children before he decided to enter Indiana State University. As a student, he worked forty hours a week at the Allis-Chalmers plant to finance his studies and support his growing family.

A third child was born while he was at ISU, which meant Joe Null struggled to make ends meet and didn't have much time to spend with his youngsters.

"I remember playing catch with David and Sam a couple of times, but I never did get a chance to work with them when they were young."

As it turned out, they may have had better careers in football, but Sam Null was happy with what each of them contributed to his basketball teams.

David Null played for his father at Edgewood, graduating in 1979. Sam played for him at Jennings County before graduating in 1988.

Coach Joe Null had been a reserve on Howard Sharpe's Gerstmeyer team in high school in the 1950s, but he never pressed either of his sons to play basketball. They developed an interest in the game from being around the gym.

Joe Null was the assistant coach at Seeger when David started coming to the gym. David would go up on the stage and listen to what Coach Gene Morrison was telling the team. (Gene Morrison is now an assistant to Joe Null at Jennings County.)

It was much the same way with Sam. But Joe Null gave his sons no special attention in the gym. "They just watched practice and had a good time," he says.

Like most brothers, David and Sam were different. Coach Null explains:

"David could watch a basketball game and pick up a lot. Sam wasn't neces-sarily a student of the game, even though he turned out to be a better ball-handler and passer."

David Null agrees: "I'm the type who learns by listening. When I went to Dad's practices, I'd listen to what he was telling the varsity kids, then I would try those things on my own.

"He didn't really sit down and show me how to shoot, or how to dribble with either hand. I picked those things up when he was teaching other kids."

David began playing organized basketball as a fifth grader at Seeger. Sam started in the intramural leagues for third and fourth graders at Edgewood.

It took David Null a week to win a starting position on the Edgewood football team, where he played both offense and defense as a freshman. That made it easier, when the football season was over, for his dad to elevate him immediately to the varsity basketball team.

"The fact he could make the football team, which I wasn't even as-sociated with, made it a little easier for me to start him as a freshman," Coach Null admits. "At six-feet-two, he was the second biggest kid we had on the squad and we needed his size."

David Null made his presence known in the first game of the season. He drew a charge to gain possession of the ball and give Edgewood the victory.

Joe Null still remembers that week. "It was a special one for David. He did a good job in our basketball game, he got a straight-A report card, attended a meeting of the Fellowship of Christian Athletes, went to Sunday School on Sunday morning, and went back to the youth meeting that night. That may not sound like a lot to some people, but I was proud enough of him that I paneled his room over the Christmas vacation.

"That's what you get," his dad told him, "for just being a good kid."

Joe Null heard very little criticism when he started his son as a freshman. "I can't say everyone was 100 percent in agreement. Whether you are playing your son, or someone else's son, there is never total agreement about what you are doing or who you should be playing. So the things that were said were kind of ignored."

David Null recalls that some sophomores did quit the team because they didn't feel it was right for a freshman to be playing ahead of them. The kids who remained on the team treated him well and were never critical.

That may have been because he, like Sam, wasn't a selfish player, Coach Null explains, adding:

"There were probably games when they'd take no more than three shots. They didn't go out and try to hog the ball or try to dominate the team. They

STRATEGY: Joe Null coached his son David at Edgewood, then his son Sam at Jennings County.

wanted to win just like all the other players.

"We didn't put in special plays for my sons and the kids realized that."

David Null remained a solid contributor for Joe Null's Edgewood teams for four years. He was the leading rebounder on most of those teams, but never the leading scorer.

"That probably made things easier for him," Joe Null says, "because the other players knew we weren't going to him on every play. He shot a good percentage, but his job was inside-rebounding and doing things most fans wouldn't recognize or remember. He played awfully, awfully good defense."

And Edgewood made progress each year David was in school, winning six games as a freshman, eleven as a sophomore, fourteen as a junior, and sixteen as a senior.

The team won nineteen games the next year, and Joe Null credits David with playing an important part in turning the Edgewood program around.

After coaching David for four years, Coach Null decided not to move Sam up to the varsity too early. Although he heard little criticism for starting David as a freshman, he "just didn't want to go through that again. Even though people don't make phone calls or talk to you about playing your son, the feeling is there."

Like other coaches he had no desire to put his son in situations he couldn't handle. That is why, he says, "I think coaches hold their sons back a little bit to make sure they are ready."

Sam Null played on the "B" team in basketball as a freshman.

That next fall he made an impact on the football team, scoring a lot of touchdowns and taking over as quarterback.

As a sophomore in basketball he played two quarters of "B" team ball and dressed for the varsity, where his dad credits him with contributing to some of the team's sixteen victories. "He just went in and got the ball where we wanted it to go."

Sam was the first player off the bench as a junior in 1986-87 on an outstanding team that was ranked in the top twenty in the state. He played a big role on a team that lost only two times all season, both to finals-bound Bedford-North Lawrence.

Meantime, Sam continued to play well in football, moving from quarterback to running back as a senior.

He became a starter at point guard on his dad's basketball team as a senior and helped lead Jennings County to an 11-10 record. After that 21-2 junior season, there was a lot of pressure for the team to finish above .500. Joe Null recalls an overtime game late in the season:

"Sam came to the bench and told Billy Harmon, one of the coaches, 'I'm going to win it at the free-throw line.' As a junior, he had not been a very good free-throw shooter, but he had worked hard to become better over the summer. But it was still something for him to say something like that."

Even more to his credit, he *did* win the game at the free-throw line.

PRESSURES: Joe Null thinks sons of coaches feel more pressure than their fathers do.

"They do not want to let their teammates or their schools down.

"Whether we like it or not, we coaches are judged by our record. So I think our sons feel the pressure whether it is there or not. No son wants to look back and think that if he had played better his family might not have had to change jobs.

"Coaches have a high desire to achieve. They can put a lot of pressure on themselves and, consequently, their kids do, too."

Coach Null realizes he put more pressure on his sons than on he did on other players.

His friends understood that. And they told him, "Hey, you are taking this too seriously. You're taking it out on David. If he makes one error, you take him out."

As Joe Null said, his two sons had different personalities: "David would feel the pressure. Sam didn't worry a heck of a lot about it, or if he did, he didn't show it outright."

WHAT THE PLAYER FEELS: David Null admits "I felt [the pressure] all the way through high school. It may have been pressure I put on myself. Dad didn't really say a lot to me about it. He didn't have to. But he would look at me and I would know what he was thinking."

Part of the pressure also came because David Null "loved the game" and wanted to play well.

Like most sons of coaches, he realized his dad put more pressure on him than other players. "He just wanted me to be the best. If I would mess up, he might really tie into me, whereas he might do more coaching than yelling at another player. He expected me to know more about the game."

David Null credits football with keeping him from getting too wrapped up in basketball. "I could have been in the gym playing basketball eight to ten hours a day if I wanted to. I could go to all the basketball games I wanted to." Football was a form of escape.

Looking back, David Null now knows he was too hard on himself in high school. "I liked basketball in junior high, but I really didn't enjoy it again until I started playing intramural games in college.

"I was afraid of making errors in high school. I just didn't want to make mistakes. I wanted to be a perfect player."

He knows it's difficult, but he suggests a coach treat his son as if he's another kid on the basketball court. And he tells sons of coaches "do the best you can. Don't think of the coach as your father. Think of him as a coach. Relax and go out there and enjoy playing the game."

WHAT THE COACH THINKS: Like other husbands, Coach Null sometimes was guilty of thinking about his job when he was at home. "Basketball might have run through my mind while my wife was trying to talk about something else. Sometimes I only half-way paid attention to what the family was doing."

His teams play in the tough Hoosier Hills conference, having to compete in the rugged Seymour sectional with Seymour and Bedford-North Lawrence.

Coaching is an intense job. "The son of a coach has to understand that. It is a job in which a father is going to do and say things he will regret a few minutes, a week, or maybe even ten years later.

"There are many times when the son of a coach may get chewed out when the love of his dad doesn't show through. The son must still realize that love is there."

FINAL THOUGHTS: Joe Null's advice for a coach who has his son as a player: "Let him play for the fun of it. Don't apply that pressure. There are just so many Steve Alfords. They all are not all going to be superstars. It's not fair to the kids to expect them to be."

"I'm proud of both the boys," Joe Null concludes. "They're fine young men."

Postscript: Joe Null is still coach at Jennings County. David Null played football at Hanover College before graduating from Indiana State. He taught and coached at Edgewood, was assistant coach at Danville, and now is an assistant basketball coach at Seymour. Sam Null is a student at Indiana State.

Out of Their Shadow

COACH AL TUCKER AND SONS BRAD AND CHAD

For years, Brad Tucker was known as Al Tucker's son, or the brother of Chad Tucker, the superstar.

He became what he wanted to be in the summer of 1989. From then on he was Brad Tucker the coach, head man for the South Knox High School basketball program. The shadows cast by his dad and brother were gone.

Sure, he was proud of his dad, a man whose Cloverdale teams won 256 games in 17 seasons, and his younger brother, Chad, who was Butler University's all-time leading scorer.

Chad Tucker understood. He sometimes said he was Brad Tucker's younger brother.

But Brad wanted basketball fans to recognize him for what he could accomplish. He wanted to make a name for himself.

As a player for his dad at Cloverdale, Brad Tucker wasn't a standout, and he might not have made the team at a bigger school. As a coach, he paid his dues, serving four years as an assistant at Madison.

By then Chad had graduated from Butler and was playing professional basketball in Taiwan. Brad visited him there in the summer of 1989, watched his games, and returned home, where he learned he had the South Knox job.

Brad was prepared for the job. Being a coach's son had helped. So did being an assistant under John Church and Don Lostutter at Madison. He had seen how three different men coach the game and he had picked up something from each of them.

But it was his dad from whom he may have learned the most: "In a way, I think I instinctively try to pattern myself after him. I try to keep a positive attitude. And I know what pressures are involved, having seen what Dad went through."

As a high school player, Brad Tucker was a role-player, a hatchet-man on defense. "I wasn't expected to score twenty points a game," he explains.

Now that he is a coach, he appreciates those type players. "I can sympathize with the ninth and tenth men," he says. "I have sat down on the bench where they are. I know how they feel."

His dad agrees Brad was a marginal player. But he also is sure that because of his persistence and perseverance he will become a better coach than he was a player.

Brad played on the varsity only as a senior, and then as the fifth and sixth man on the squad. "You could depend on what he was going to do," Al Tucker says. "He wasn't much of a scorer, but he handled the ball fairly well and he was a thinker. He was the kind of player you had to utilize in a small school."

Brad Tucker, nevertheless, made a lot of contributions to the overall program, his dad adds. "He was happy to play and he didn't have to score to be content. It is an asset to have a kid who is happy to play and isn't interested in personal statistics."

CHAD TUCKER: Brad Tucker graduated from Cloverdale in 1980, the year Chad entered high school as a freshman. As a junior-high player, Chad was one of the better players on the team, but not the best.

It would become apparent to Coach Al Tucker that season that Chad could be a superstar. "By the end of the year it was obvious he had an instinct for the game and that he would have some size."

Al Tucker recalls, "We had a talk before the season was out. He asked me what I thought he would have to do to play varsity ball the next year. I wrote down a regimentation—rope jumping, shooting and conditioning—and said, 'Do this and I'm not going to check on you. But I'll know whether you do it or not.'"

He didn't have to check on him. Chad played three nights a week at school and never missed a single day doing what his dad asked him to do.

Chad and Jerry Neese, another sophomore, moved into the varsity lineup the next season. The first game ended in an overtime, with Tucker and Neese scoring all the points in the extra period to give the Clovers the victory.

That ended any doubts fans had about whether Al Tucker was showing favoritism to his son Chad, and his pal Jerry Neese, by starting them as sophomores.

It would be the first of a long run of successes for Cloverdale. That year the Clovers went to the regional and closed the season with a 22-3 record. The next year the team went undefeated until the regional for a 24-1 record. When Chad Tucker was a senior, bigger schools were added to the schedule and the team finished 21-7.

That gave Cloverdale a three-year record of 67-11, which isn't bad in any league.

By his senior year, Chad Tucker had grown to 6'5". He averaged 24.5 points and 10 rebounds a game as a senior and was named to the 1983 Indiana All-Star team.

He went on to Butler where he made the All-Midwestern Collegiate Conference team three times, averaging 24.1 points a game as a senior.

LEARNING THE GAME: Al Tucker never forced basketball on Brad, Chad, or daughter Dawn or insisted that they excel at the sport. But that didn't stop them from becoming gym rats. They grew up around basketball and spent a lot of time at the gym, although Al Tucker never let them or other players work out unless he was there.

Brad and Chad were allowed to ride the bus to away games as youngsters. But they could only ride back to Cloverdale if the team won. "If we lost," Al Tucker explains, "I didn't want them there because it was a different type of atmosphere."

Al and his wife, Joan, built a new home in 1973 and the concrete for the basketball court was poured and the goal erected before the house was completed. On that court the Tucker kids would spend hours on end playing basketball with their friends. "It would be," Al Tucker says, "the best investment I ever made."

Al Tucker saw to it his kids had competition at a very early age. "I presented things to them in the form of a challenge. We tried to make a competitive game out of shooting and other type drills. That helped them maintain their interest."

"I was in the palace of basketball, and there was my son, an Indiana All-Star."

ON HIS OWN: Brad Tucker (left) played for his dad, Al, and came out of the shadow of his superstar brother to coach at South Knox

THE PRESSURES: "I tried not to put any extra pressure on my kids, or use them as examples," Al Tucker says. "I may have unconsciously done it, but I certainly didn't intend to. In talking with my kids, I told them, 'This may not be fair to you, but you're going to have to accept it because this is the way it's going to be. If it comes down to whether you're going to be the fifth or sixth man, you'll be the sixth man, because you are my son. I'm doing this to protect you, number one, and it may make you play better, and, number two, to protect myself.'"

Tucker warns parents not to put too much pressure on their youngsters to play. "Some fathers, who weren't too good themselves, want their kids to be stars so they can live out their fantasies through them."

There also can be pressure for the wife of a coach. Joan Tucker sat on the side opposite the Cloverdale fans at home games to avoid hearing what was being said about her sons or her husband.

And there can even be resentment from some teachers. "They sometimes are jealous or resentful of coaches because a coach makes more money, or because of the publicity they receive," Al Tucker says.

That may be why one or two teachers kept Chad Tucker from being on the Honor Society, even though he was qualified.

Despite the pressures, as Brad Tucker starts his head coaching career he has thought about whether he would like to coach a son some day. And he concludes he would.

A TUCKER VIGNETTE: Chad Tucker and Jerry Neese were superior performers on Al Tucker's 1982-83 team and he gave them some freedom he wouldn't give other players. They liked to use some fancy behind-the-back passes and Coach Tucker gave them permission to do so with the understanding that they would be yanked out of the game if the passes didn't connect, no matter whose fault it was.

In a game against Southmont, Chad made a major-league pass behind his back to another kid, who fumbled the ball out of bounds. Without having to be told, Chad walked over to the bench and sat down.

Some fans didn't understand why he had taken himself out of the game. But it wasn't lost on the Southmont school superintendent. He told Coach Al Tucker after the game: "That was the classiest act I have ever seen on a basketball floor. Your son knew your rule. He knew the consequences, and he accepted them. I want to commend you and him for it."

A MOMENT TO REMEMBER: Al Tucker was born in Kentucky but came to Indiana and graduated from Patricksburg High School. It gave him a special thrill when he sat in the 24,000-seat Rupp Arena at Lexington, Kentucky, and saw his son Chad circling the playing floor with the 1983 Indiana All-Stars.

"I was in Rupp Arena, the palace of basketball, and there was my son out on the floor, an Indiana All-Star."

Postscript: Al Tucker quit coaching at Cloverdale in 1984 to become a State Farm Insurance representative in Greencastle. Tucker says he misses coaching, especially at the beginning of the season and when the Indiana state basketball tournament starts.

Earning Bragging Rights

COACH STEVE DEGROOTE AND SONS CORY, CULLEY, AND CASEY

Right off, Steve DeGroote admits he likes to brag on players he coaches. It's a confidence-building elixir he brought from Iowa and has used at West Vigo to rebuild a down-and-out basketball program into a force to be reckoned with in the Terre Haute area.

As a former college football star who signed a pro contract with the Minnesota Vikings, he doesn't need a supporting cast. But he has his own "C-force"—his wife, Connie, a winning coach herself; Cory, a sophomore starter on his 1988-89 West Vigo team; Culley, who was in the seventh grade; Casey, a fourth grader, and Cami, a second grader.

Steve DeGroote brags on his West Vigo team, he brags on his own sons, and, as a coach, he can boast about the accomplishments that come when pride replaces doubt.

Building confidence was his first objective at West Vigo, a job he took after resigning as assistant coach of the Indiana State University baseball team.

"I bragged on the kids that were there. Some people told me that I shouldn't do that, that the kids might not be able to live up to my expectations of them."

That didn't bother DeGroote, even though West Vigo hadn't had a winning team in years. He saw talent and potential. "It was up to me to refine that potential and to instill confidence in the players.

"I knew I could win there because I knew I'd work their [the players'] fannies off if that was what it took."

Whatever it took, DeGroote found it. His first team finished the season 15-7 and lost the sectional championship, 68-66, to a tough Terre Haute

North team. West Vigo followed that up with a 16-6 season in 1987-88, and in the 1988-89 season the Vikings won a school-record twelve games in a row, finishing 17-6 with a loss to highly-ranked Terre Haute South.

That gave DeGroote's first three West Vigo teams a 48-19 record, and, he added, optimistic as usual, "It'll be even better next season [1989-90]." And chances are the former Iowa farm boy will see to it, "by gum!"

1988-89 was DeGroote's most rewarding season in coaching. "I had lost starters that were six-feet-six, six-feet-five, six-feet-three, and six-feet-two. I came back with three kids under six feet, one just over six feet and my son Cory, who was a six-feet-four sophomore."

Cory, who had played some varsity ball as a freshman, averaged 11.2 points, 8.2 rebounds, and 4.6 assists as a sophomore, giving his dad more bragging rights.

THE BOYS AS PLAYERS: DeGroote returned to high school coaching so he could spend more time with Cory, Culley, and Casey.

Cory DeGroote got his first taste of basketball back in Iowa, where his dad coached before coming to Indiana State.

"Iowa didn't have organized ball in the lower grades like Indiana, but Cory came to the gym and some of my players took to him," his dad recalls.

"Our kids wore ties and suits to games and Cory had to have one, too. He walked into the gym with the team. He could have had no better role models."

Cory, Culley and Casey have all picked up a lot about basketball from being around the gym. They chose players as idols, mimicked their expressions, copied their shots, and duplicated their gestures.

They sat with the team on the bench, acted as statisticians, and went scouting with their dad.

It is important, Coach DeGroote says, for high school players to remember that there are younger players watching, wanting to emulate them. The examples they set must be positive.

Steve DeGroote enrolled nine-year-old Cory in the Boys Club league when he arrived in Terre Haute. It provided, he says, a structured program with good coaching and a clean environment.

Steve also did some coaching at home. "I'm really nuts on fundamentals. I tell the kids to forget it if they think they are just going to play games. We start with footwork, dribbling, passing, shooting. Some people try to teach kids to run plays at an early age. I teach kids to dribble, pass, and shoot."

He made sure the goal in his garage was low enough so his sons, and their friends, could dunk the ball. "At that height they can slam the ball on offense or slap it away on defense. After two to three hours, they may have jumped 1,000 times. If the goal was higher they might have jumped just 100

COMPETITORS ALL: West Vigo Coach Steve DeGroote (upper right) and sons (counterclockwise) Cory, Culley, and Casey

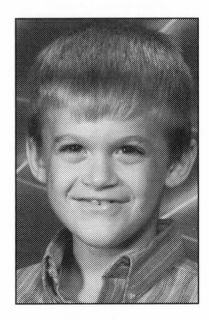

times," he says, explaining his reasoning.

"They can't wait until they are seventeen years old to learn to jump and block shots and do the other skills," he adds.

Cory progressed as a player through junior high and started on the Jayvee team as a freshman, when he also played in a few varsity games.

"If he hadn't been my son, he might have played more," Coach De-Groote confesses.

If there was any jealousy about Cory DeGroote playing on the varsity as a freshman, Coach DeGroote didn't hear it: "Everyone was positive."

When Cory was introduced as a varsity starter as a sophomore, the fans cheered for him as loudly as for the other players. And his teammates accepted him.

His dad had told him, "You are my son. There is no way around that. But the worst thing I can do is favor you as my son. If I do, you'll be a marked man. I'm going to jump on you so hard so many times it will be unbelievable.

"I was extra-hard on Cory," he says. "I think a lot of times, when he didn't hear a good word out of me, that the other kids came to his defense."

He admits he doesn't praise Cory enough or tell him how great a job he does. "Instead, I am always seeking higher grounds for him."

When Cory earned his place on the team, Steve DeGroote could look ahead to what Culley and Casey might be able to accomplish. And he isn't hesitant to brag about them, either.

Culley is, he boasts, "as smooth as silk. He has a chance, with good work habits, to be fantastic. He can handle the ball, he can pass, and he can pull up and pop it. He'll nail you with a three-pointer."

It is a bit too early to tell about Casey, but his dad says he, too, can go up for a jump-shot and "pop."

A BIT OF PHILOSOPHY: Steve DeGroote uses a bit of psychology on his team. "I pick a kid out every once in a while. I tell him before the season starts that he is my leader and that I'm going to nail him at times. I tell him there will be days when I eat him alive.

"The others see what's going on and know that the star is getting his fanny chewed. They know then that there are no prima donnas on the team.

Another DeGroote tenet: "I never pick a most-valuable player, I never will. You never will hear me play up a player. Big scoring nights cannot be accomplished without someone getting the ball to the shooters.

"I never single out a kid and my players know it. I think if you are a successful coach you have to love every one of those kids to death.

"They know I'm available twenty-four hours a day. They know they can call me at two a.m. if they are in any kind of trouble."

WIFE AND MOTHER: Connie DeGroote, too, has been around basketball all her life. Her father, Demps Christensen, was a great athlete in Iowa, and she says she grew up on a concrete basketball court.

She also played softball; her team at Twin Rivers (Iowa) High School went to the state finals. She has two brothers, Mike and Dennis Christensen, and a sister, Susie Kalsow, all of whom coach in Iowa.

Mrs. DeGroote coached the West Vigo junior high girls' team to a county championship after the family moved to Indiana.

"With Cory," she says, "my role is one of being supportive. With Steve it is being an understanding wife. I'm a good listener. I guess the main thing for both of them is that I am there when they need me."

REVERSE FAVORITISM: Steve DeGroote has heard this story about a coach's conversation with a player:

"You better be awfully good because you are going to be competing against my son. And you ought to know that I love my son. So you had better be a lot better."

He doubts a coach would have had such a conversation. It usually works the other way.

"I think coaches puts more pressure on their sons than on other players. We are just too critical some times. We want our son to be greater than the others."

Some parents, however, want their sons to be great individual players and aren't concerned about the other players. "As a coach," Steve DeGroote explains, "I want all five players to be great individuals, but I am more concerned about them being a great team."

COACH, PLAYER; FATHER, SON: It is tough, Coach DeGroote admits, to separate the father and coach roles.

"Once you get on the practice floor, personal is out. Cory is just another player. That's the way it has to be.

"I know it is rough on him to be chewed out by the coach, who also is his father. A lot of times a kid leaves a game with his dad's arm around him. Cory leaves with a dad who has just chewed on him.

"Once we leave, I, too, have to be a father. As his coach, I have to tell him that he can be a better ballplayer. As his father I have to tell him I'm proud as heck of him."

With two more sons coming up through the grades, a lot of coaching, a lot of loving . . . and a lot of bragging are ahead for Coach Steve DeGroote.

A Family Affair

COACH GLENN ANDREW AND SONS BOBBY AND BRETT

Before his children were born, Glenn Andrew decided he wanted to coach high school basketball.

"Coaching is my occupation, an occupation I chose. It just so happened that my sons were born, became interested in basketball, and played for me because I chose that as my profession."

The result has worked out well.

For Andrew and his wife, Carol, basketball is a family affair centered around North Central High School at Farmersburg in Sullivan County.

Their oldest son, Bobby, played there. Daughter Rhonda made her mark on the girls' team. Son Brett joined the varsity as a freshman in the 1988-89 season. And Shannon, the youngest of the Andrew children, is looking forward to a junior high career.

It's natural for Glenn Andrew's offspring to like basketball. He played at Rockville High School and later, after getting married and starting a family, at Huntington College. After averaging 16 points a game at Huntington he returned to the Terre Haute area and played independent basketball, at times with Larry Bird.

Andrew's family was growing by that time and his wife would pack the diapers and keep one eye on her toddlers, the other on her husband on the floor.

That exposure, thanks to Carol Andrew's patience, helped the Andrew youngsters develop an interest in basketball.

Coach Andrew says he made no special effort to make his sons basketball players. But he does concede that shortly after Bobby was brought home from the hospital, he had a goal in his crib. Brett, too, had a goal at a young age.

Andrew started helping his boys with their shooting techniques when they each were about four years old. "I made them use a smaller ball so they could handle it properly."

Each son started playing basketball when he was five years old in the Boys Club at Terre Haute, a place many future stars learned the game.

BOBBY ANDREW: Glenn Andrew decided to move his family to Farmersburg during Bobby's sixth-grade year, giving Bobby his first exposure to the North Central school system.

"I was scared to death," he says. "I had never been to school with the kids, had never been to school here at all. There I was, at basketball practice.

They didn't know me and already I was Bobby, the son of the coach."

It was at North Central where Bobby first started taking the game seriously. By then, he knew he wouldn't be very tall and that he would have to learn to handle the ball and develop a shot if he wanted to play.

Bobby Andrew had to work hard for what he accomplished in basketball. He wasn't a natural athlete, a fact both he and his dad recognized. That he had studied the game would become his biggest asset.

"As point guard," Coach Andrew says, "he was my coach on the floor. He knew where to get the ball and how to get it there. He was unselfish."

He had trouble hitting layups as a freshman, his dad recalls. "He would come to the gym for hours at a time and shoot nothing but layups. I remember once as a sophomore when he was on the "B" team when he missed a layup on an uncontested break-away.

"He came out of the game almost in tears and said, 'I practiced so hard not to miss a layup and I missed one.' I told him just keep shooting. I don't think he missed one from then on."

Bobby became a starter on the varsity as a junior, which he recalls as a trying transition. He thinks he deserved to play earlier. "But I realized my dad was in a tough situation. He had to make sure I was ready and that I deserved to play.

"I had been coming off the bench and playing quite a bit. That didn't seem to have bothered anyone. Now, all of a sudden, I had moved into a starting role, taking a senior's position. People just didn't know quite how to react.

"When I was introduced, they didn't boo. They just weren't sure how to react. They didn't clap or scream or go crazy like they did for some of the other players."

He started every game from then on, but it would be some time before everyone was convinced: "I took a lot of heat from a couple of the other players. But I was ready for that. I knew it was going to come. It didn't bother me to hear it. It did bother me when fans carried it to the point where they were making a scene and creating concern to my mom, my brother, and my sisters."

Bobby Andrew considered the source of the complaints and told himself: "You guys are in the stands booing and I'm out here playing basketball. That shows something about the individuals involved."

He decided to prove he deserved to play. "Right after the sectional game, I set a goal for myself that as a senior I was going to be Bob the player, not Bob the coach's son. I had that printed and posted in different places so I would always remember it."

He spent the summer improving his game. "I lifted weights every other

HANGING OUT:
North Central Coach
Glenn Andrew with
sons Bobby and
(topside) Brett

day, I ran, shot, and worked on ball-handling. When school started that fall I was ready to play basketball. I was ready to prove to these people that I deserved to play.

"When the first game of the 1985-86 season came, I ran onto the floor, thinking, 'This is it. This is where it starts.' It was just totally different. I was accepted by my teammates as Bob the player. The attitude of the students and fans was totally different. It was a different atmosphere."

And it was the year the team looked to him for leadership. He had established himself as a player and as a leader.

Bobby Andrew opted not to play basketball at Wabash College. He decided instead to be a student assistant, a role in which he helped with recruiting and scouting and got to do a little floor-coaching.

Despite that experience, Bobby Andrew doesn't want to coach. "I'm not going to expose my family to the things our family has been exposed to. I don't mean that to be selfish. I just don't want to go through it. I can handle the criticism. But I think it is unfair for a family to have to do it."

He is a communications major in college and eventually plans on a public-relations career, possibly in motor sports.

BRETT ANDREW: Brett Andrew played a lot of basketball before he reached high school. In one year, Brett played seventy-plus games, counting those in school, in the summer, in the Boys Club leagues, and on all-star teams in Terre Haute. Almost from the time Brett first held a basketball, his father thought he might develop into a good player. He had long arms and big hands.

And he continued to grow. He may have been ready for the varsity at the start of the 1988-89 season when he was a freshman. Coach Andrew, however, moved with caution. He assigned his son to the "B" team.

He knew he probably would have started Bobby on the varsity earlier if he hadn't been his son. And he was convinced he wouldn't let that happen with Brett. Still, Glenn Andrew says, "I had people tell me I was dumb for not playing Brett on the varsity at the start of his freshman year. But he wasn't ready mentally or [mature enough], so we waited until we thought the time was right. We didn't want to hurt him or the team by bringing him up before he was ready."

Brett was moved up to varsity about mid-January of his freshman year. "He played quite a bit and helped us out considerably from his guard position," dad Andrew says. At 6'2" he already was taller than Bobby was as a senior, and Coach Andrew, who is 6'4" himself, figures Brett may be at least 6'5" when he graduates in 1992.

AT HOME: "You say you don't take the game home," Glenn Andrew says. "Yet, it's like anything else. If you are a professional in your line of work, it's hard not to take it home. You try not to, but basketball is a big part of our lives."

He does try to refrain from talking about the game at meals. And he tries not to talk at home after a bad outing. "I might say some things I shouldn't be saying. . . . But it's hard not to ask, 'Brett, why didn't you do this or that?'

"Any coach who says he doesn't instruct his son outside the two hours of practice at the gym is lying. Other kids have fathers who give them lots of advice. The advice I give my son is what he will need to apply in practice the next night. The advice parents give might be just the opposite of what I am trying to accomplish."

Coach Andrew talked to men who had experienced coaching their sons. "They all told me not to make it hard on your own kid, not to use him as an example, and to try to treat him like anyone else."

He adds, "I tried not to say at halftime, 'Bobby, you dummy. Why didn't you do this or that?' Now there are times when I did that, but I tried not to do it. I don't do that to my other players. We try to critique them in a way that we feel it should be done."

THE CRITICISM: Criticism is a problem for any coach who has his son as a player. "You can say it isn't a problem," Glenn Andrew relates, "but it is there, maybe a little more today than it was years ago. The parental viewpoint of athletes is different than years ago. There are some parents who'd rather their kid play and the team lose than for someone else's kids to play and you win."

That, he says, is one of the biggest changes he has noticed in fifteen years of coaching.

SORRY, WRONG NUMBER: Like all fathers, Glenn Andrew sometimes has trouble keeping his youngsters straight.

The first game Brett played resulted in a technical foul. Coach Andrew explains what happened:

"We had two different numbers for our home and away uniforms. Brett was No. 12 in white and No. 14 in green. We played at Riverton Parke and were wearing green. For some reason, when I made out the scorebook, I thought Brett is going to wear No. 50, just like Rhonda did. So I wrote 50 beside his name."

When Andrew put his son into the game in the second quarter, the referee came over and said, "There is a technical foul on No. 14. His number is not in the book."

Coach Andrew adds, "What a way for a coach's son to start his varsity career."

North Central went ahead to win the game anyway. Brett didn't score in his debut, but he did a good job off the boards, played good defense, and had some good passes off the fast break.

RHONDA ANDREW: Rhonda Andrew offers no apology for wanting to follow in her father's footsteps. She wants to coach and teach business, just like he does. And she still is a big fan of her dad, her brother Brett, and the North Central team.

She confesses, "Probably half of our conversations are about basketball when I come home from college on weekends. We may stay up until two a.m. on Friday and Saturday nights talking about who is doing well and all that kind of stuff."

If she has a daughter, would she like to coach her? "I think I would. I know it might cause trouble, but I'd just want her to be the best she could be, and as her coach I could see that she was."

Would she use her dad as a guide? "Definitely."

WIFE AND MOTHER: Carol Andrew is librarian at Farmersburg Elementary School. With four children and a husband involved in sports, there is little time for anything other than athletics.

Being the mother of players and the wife of a coach, you might expect that she sometimes has to be a referee at home. "I voice my opinion, but they never listened to me," she said, underrating herself.

She and Glenn never talk about the criticism and the complaints of fans in front of the kids. "If I tell him what someone has said, I'd wait until we are alone."

The Andrews had worried that too much exposure might sour their children against basketball, especially Shannon, because she had been exposed to it all her life through her older sister and brothers.

"But," Carol Andrew adds, "she is going to be as involved as the others."

Carol Andrew has no big disappointments about her role as wife and mother. "It gets more difficult for me, though. The complaining from fans is the hardest part. I don't like to hear fans complain. Otherwise I love it."

A QUICK DIVERSION: Glenn Andrew drives his own Sports Car Club of America car in competition on tracks at Indianapolis Raceway Park in Indianapolis, St. Louis, Detroit, Cleveland, and Elkhart Lake.

He has done well, crew manager Bobby Andrew says, even though the race team doesn't have a lot of financial support. "We are competitive so we feel successful even though we know we are not going to win. We just go out and have fun . . . and that's what it is all about."

SOMETHING TO REMEMBER: The coach-player relationship is one neither Glenn, Bobby, or Brett Andrew will forget. The hugs on the floor after victories. The tears in the locker room after defeats. "Those things will be with us the rest of our lives," Coach Andrew concludes.

A Coach and a Smile

COACH DAN BUSH AND SON ALAN BUSH

Alan Bush was one of the top players on the 1988-89 unbeaten freshman team at Bedford-North Lawrence High School. He was being interviewed on the school's television station.

He was asked: "Assuming you make the varsity next season, how will you feel about playing for your dad [Coach Dan Bush]?"

Alan replied: "Well, let me put it this way. The other players just have him two or three hours a day. I have to go home with him."

He did not elaborate. He had inherited his father's southern Indiana wit. And, chances are, he knew he would hear about basketball at home as well as in the gym.

It is that way for a lot of coaches' sons.

* * *

Dan Bush had watched his son progress as a player from grade school through his freshman year, and he knew he probably was ready to move onto the varsity when the next season arrived.

He tried to prepare himself for what to expect. He talked with other coaches who had sons as players, seeking insights, opinions, and advice. Some told him it would be an enjoyable experience. Others said it might be unpleasant at times. Some told him they never talked basketball with their sons outside the gym. Others said they talked about it all the time.

It was obvious to Coach Bush he would have to decide for himself what path the relationship would take. But he knew he wanted to treat Alan as he would any other player. "I'll try not to do anything different," he said.

A GYM RAT GROWS UP: It was only natural that Alan Bush become a gym rat. His dad had been an outstanding player at Indiana State University after leaving Oolitic High School, where he scored 1,467 points and led his team to an unbeaten season.

By the time Alan was two years old, his dad had mounted a goal on the basement wall four to five feet off the floor. Alan was ecstatic when he learned to dunk the ball at that height.

Alan started coming to the gym when he was four years old. "Any coach's son who wants to spend time with his dad will be in the gym a lot," Dan Bush explains. When the team was playing full-court in practice, Alan

Bush would shoot on the end opposite the action, then hurry out of the way as the players rushed back down-court.

Alan spent hours out on the floor, especially after practices. Older players shot with him and became his idols and role models. He had an opportunity to be around great teams. In the three seasons before the start of the 1989-90 campaign, his dad's teams had a 70-8 record, including two trips to the state finals.

Like most sons of coaches, Alan picked up knowledge other kids don't have a chance to learn. "That's why a lot of coaches play their sons," Dan Bush explains. "There may be criticism. But they are playing because they know what is going on."

Alan Bush was in the first grade when he started playing biddy ball at the Boys Club in Bedford. He continued to play through the grades, was on the Oolitic junior high team, and then moved onto the freshman team at Bedford-North Lawrence. He played AAU basketball in the summer of 1989.

Other than teaching him the correct shooting technique, Dan Bush never gave his son specialized instructions until the summer between his eighth-grade and freshman seasons. His dad explains, "I was too busy working with everyone else's kids."

Coach Bush notes Alan "improved 150 percent" from that time through the summer of 1989. The coach spent a lot of time with his son at the gym, but he adds, "I've spent a lot of time out here with other kids, too."

As head coach, Dan Bush could have advised the freshman coach how to handle Alan, but that's not his style. "I didn't have any role in what Alan did. I let the freshman coach coach him.

"The only thing I asked Alan to do was to play as hard as he could. If he plays as hard as he can, he may have nights when the ball won't go in the basket. I understand that, but I just want him to play as hard as he can."

Alan averaged about fifteen points a game and shot between 55 and 60 percent from the field and 80 percent from the free-throw line on a freshman team that had a 21-0 record.

Some of Alan's fans and friends suggested to Coach Bush that he elevate his son to the Jayvee team. He explained why he didn't: "Alan was in a position where he was playing all the time at the freshman level and had a lot of success. I thought we'd just leave him there and that he'd get enough experience to make the varsity as a sophomore. I wanted to make sure he got his playing time in. Our freshman coaches do a real good job and they wanted to win the [Hoosier Hills] Conference tournament. So I just let him stay down."

THE FUTURE: As the 1989-90 season approached, Dan Bush looked forward to having his son join Damon Bailey, Jamie Cummings, Jason Lam-

*"Any coach's son who wants to spend time
with his dad will be in the gym a lot."
    —Coach Dan Bush, on son Alan (below),
        now a player at Bedford-North Lawrence*

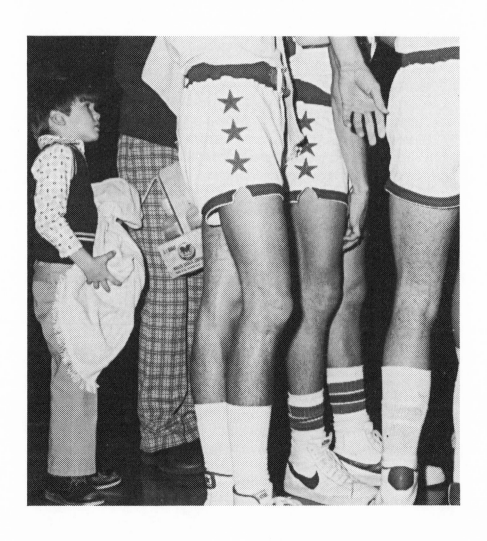

brecht, and other upperclassmen on the B-NL varsity.

"I hope he is ready," his dad says. "I think he can play."

He planned to treat his son as he would any other player. "I'll try not to do anything different. But I'll probably be more critical of him than the others. I imagine I will expect more from him. I was brought up with the philosophy that you get what you expect. If you don't expect much, you won't get much."

And he admits he has been pretty tough on Alan. "If he's not playing as hard as I'd like for him to play, I tell him.

"He's a good shooter. In fact, he's one of the best we have had around here. He sees the floor well and handles the ball well, shoots the ball exceptionally well."

Alan Bush was on a weight program four days a week before his sophomore season to build up his upper-body strength, one of the few weaknesses his dad observed might hurt his play.

Alan Bush knows that if he doesn't want to play hard, he won't be on the floor. That's one of Bush's rules, not only for his son but for any other player on the team.

A GAME OF INTANGIBLES: Dan Bush knows a coach takes a lot of heat sometimes because he plays his son. But he also knows basketball is a game of intangibles. It's not like golf where a kid who shoots a 74 consistently is obviously better than one who shoots a 77.

"The five best one-on-one players don't necessarily make the best team," Dan Bush explains. "A lot of people don't understand that. I've had five kids on the bench who could beat the five kids on the floor one-on-one.

"Some kids may be good shooters, others good defensive players, others good passers, others good ball-handlers. So, I tell my teams it is not the best five one-on-one players, it's the five players who mesh together into the best team who will play."

And Bush says he doesn't need statistics to tell him who is playing well. "Anybody who knows anything about the game doesn't need them, either."

That is why he keeps telling Alan how important it is to play hard. "If there are nights when his shots aren't going in, there are other things he will have to do well. That's why Damon Bailey is so doggoned good. If his shot is not going in, he still does other things so well. Damon wouldn't have to score a point and he would help his team."

BEYOND THE GAME: Dan and Carol Bush have told their son that basketball is important, but that he is a student first, a player second. He made the A Honor Roll as a freshman.

He also played on the baseball team. His dad says Alan may enjoy baseball because, "There isn't as much pressure as there is in basketball. And he's not the coach's son."

ANECDOTES: The Bedford-North Lawrence team was en route home after the 1987 state finals, having been beaten by state-champion Marion. Alan Bush was seated next to Damon Bailey, the super-freshman on that team. The two were bantering back and forth, as they often do.

It was a time before Dan Bush knew how good his son could be. And it was the year before the three-point shot became part of high school basketball.

Alan Bush announced, "When I start playing, it'll be the B & B boys, Bailey and Bush."

Coach Bush turned, and, using his own brand of humor, said, "No more than Alan will be playing, that'll be kind of hard to get done."

Alan looked at his father and replied, "Shoot, with that three-point shot coming in you can't afford to keep me on the bench."

Damon Bailey still reminds Alan Bush of that conversation. And as Alan Bush prepared for his varsity debut, Bailey sometimes jokingly reminded him he would need to be a passer as well as a shooter. Case in point:

The bleachers in the B-NL gym were rolled up one day in the summer of 1989 with the numbers of rows showing in descending order, 9-8-7-6-5-4-3-2-1. Bailey, whose jersey number was 32, pointed to the numbers and told young Bush: "Take a good look at the 3 and the 2. You should spend a lot of time throwing the ball between those two numbers, because that's what you are going to be doing next season."

Alan Bush relished the jesting and looked ahead to his varsity debut.

Postscript: The final chapters in the Dan and Alan Bush relationship remain to be written. Chances are when those chapters are completed and Alan Bush graduates in 1992, it will be another story of a father-son who made the transition to coach-player a pleasant experience.

The Unkindest Cuts of All

COACH PAT RADY

Pat Rady was home after what was one of the hardest days of the year for him or any other basketball coach.

He had made his final cuts from candidates for his 1985-86 Terre Haute South team. It had been as trying for him as for the players who did not make the team.

The phone rang. It was the father of one of the boys: "I want to talk to you about my son being cut from the team."

"Fine," says Rady. "I know what you are going through. I have a son in the next room who is unhappy about being cut from the team tonight, too."

The caller hesitated. "Oh? You cut your own son from the team?"

"Yes, I did."

The man was surprised. "I guess we don't have anything to talk about," he said, and ended the conversation.

It had been tough to cut his son Patrick, a sophomore. But Rady did it again two years later when he cut his younger son, Mike, from the team.

There were some tears shed at the Rady household when he made those cuts, and he acknowledges he has had some second thoughts. Both sons, he said, could have been tenth, eleventh or twelfth men on the squads.

But coaches, he agrees, tend to be harder on their sons than on other players. "We expect more. We really do," and adds, "I have kept kids with less talent than my sons had."

"I didn't want to relive my life through my sons. I have seen coaches and parents do that."
—Pat Rady, who cut his sons from his Terre Haute South squad

Coaches' sons have some advantages in basketball. But being the coach's sons hurt Patrick and Mike. "It is important that kids get a good start. They got hurt by me moving. If kids stay in the same feeder system, they have a greater opportunity to play."

And had he been coaching at a smaller school, they would have been able to make the teams there.

Yet, Rady never told his sons he wanted them to be basketball players. "I didn't want to relive my life through them. I have seen coaches and parents do that. That may have driven me away from doing it.

"I have seen men dominate their kids' lives, forcing them into playing. I never made them feel like they had to play."

Other things in their lives were more important to Rady. "I'm happier that they are free of drugs, and things of that nature."

The experience didn't sour Patrick's desire to be a basketball coach, though. And Mike considered trying out for the team again as a senior at the start of the 1989-90 season.

Postscript: Through the 1988-89 season, Pat Rady's teams had won 409 games, lost 182. His 1988-89 Terre Haute South team was ranked No. 1 in the state for much of the season. He coached the Indiana All-Stars in the two-game series against Kentucky in 1989.

Coaching a Legend

COACH SAM ALFORD AND SONS STEVE AND SEAN

Let's set the stage. It is the last regular-season game for New Castle and the Trojans have an insurmountable lead.

Sam Alford is the coach. His older son, Steve, is on the floor. His younger son, Sean, is on the bench, in a varsity uniform for the first time.

The clock winds down to about two minutes to play. Coach Alford summons Sean, gives some instructions, and sends him into the game.

New Castle has the ball out-of-bounds, Sean comes off a pick, takes a pass from Steve, and, sinks the shot. A storybook ending!

It may have been Sam Alford's proudest moment as a father and his greatest satisfaction in six years coaching his sons.

"In Steve, I have a son who was Mr. Basketball, who scored 57 points in a semistate game, who won an Olympic gold medal in 1984, who won a

Sports Festival gold medal, who was on an NCAA national championship team, who was MVP four years at Indiana University, and who now plays in the NBA."

Sam Alford is proud of all of Steve's accomplishments. But if he had one moment to recapture, it would be that time back in 1983.

Sean Alford had been brought up for that one game from the "B" team, where he wasn't a starter. "I didn't know whether I would be criticized for that and I really didn't care at that point," Coach Alford said. "It was the only opportunity Steve and Sean would ever have to play together at New Castle."

SETTING A STANDARD: A lot of coaches who have had their sons as players in the last five years have turned to Sam Alford for advice. His name comes up in most conversations. A number of coaches sought his counsel before their sons moved into the varsity lineup.

In letters Steve Alford has clued sons of coaches about what it will be like when they play for their dads. Chances are Sean has shared his knowledge, too.

Sam Alford can talk to coaches from two viewpoints. "I had one son [Steve], who worked extremely hard and put in as many hours as a young man could put in the game.

"I had another son [Sean], who had a love for the game and enjoyed it but was not obsessed with it like Steve was.

"I admired everything Steve has accomplished simply because he did it through hard work. He was, and still is, a very dedicated player. Seldom does a day go by when he doesn't run, lift weights, shoot, or play in games. He's very dedicated to the game. So in his case he has earned everything that he has accomplished.

"Sean did an excellent job for us at New Castle and received a scholarship to Georgia Southern. He decided he didn't enjoy being Steve Alford's little brother. He didn't exactly enjoy the hours, the hard work, everything that it took to play collegiate basketball at the Division I level. He returned to Indiana, entered IU, and plays in the intramural and city leagues, where he can relax and enjoy being Sean."

Today, they still compliment one another. "Steve is a big fan of Sean and Sean is a big fan of Steve," Sam Alford explains.

STEVE, THE GYM RAT: Steve Alford was the epitome of a gym rat. "He was there all the time," his dad recalls. "Anytime I went to the gym, he went too."

By the time Steve was three years old, he was sitting beside his dad on the bench at Monroe City, where Sam Alford had his first coaching job. When Sam came home from school at 3:00 p.m., Steve would have his game outfit on and be ready to go to the game that night.

Until he graduated from high school, he missed but two games, once when he had chicken pox, once when he was in a free-throw tournament.

Sam Alford recalls Steve shooting ping-pong balls into empty peanut-butter jars and tennis balls into wastebaskets.

"He would go in his closet, close the door and stay by the hour. We'd hear him thud the tennis balls into the wastebasket and 'broadcast' the games.

"He just loved to play ball, and he could occupy his own time. He didn't need a group of people around. All we had to do was to give him a ball and a wastebasket and he would be happy."

He learned to count by keeping score at games. He'd take a clipboard and each time the scoreboard changed, he would mark down the numbers.

Steve Alford absorbed a lot about the game. He was always in the dressing room, listening and learning.

It was obvious early that Steve would be a good shooter. "He had a soft touch, if there is such a touch," his dad explains. "We didn't know how strong, how big, how quick he would be, though."

Steve had a number of big games up through junior high school, once scoring 34 points as an eighth grader.

STEVE THE PLAYER: When Steve Alford moved into high school as a freshman, Coach Alford was, as he describes, "walking on egg shells."

"I did a very poor job. I'll be the first to admit that. I didn't know how to handle the situation and I didn't do a good job with him during his freshman year. I probably should have brought him up to the varsity from Day One and played him. If I had it to do over again that's probably what I would do.

"But I brought him up, took him down, played him "B" team, played him varsity. It was back and forth. It was tough for him, it was tough for me, it was tough for everyone involved."

As in all rabid basketball cities, fans in New Castle had their own thoughts. There were fans who told Sam Alford, "You must be nuts. That kid will never play a game in the North Central Conference."

Steve endured "you can't" well. Throughout his career, he has changed those "can't do's" to "can do's."

Each time Coach Alford sent freshman Alford into a game, fans booed. But fans are fickle. By the time Steve Alford was a senior, fans were booing the coach each time he took his son *out*. Steve was accepted after his freshman year, with good reason. He average 18.5 points a game as a sophomore, 27.5 as a junior, and 37.5 as a senior.

Despite all that, Sam Alford knows of one man in New Castle who swears his son would have been an Indiana All-Star if Steve hadn't been allowed to shoot all the time. It was more proof that neither a coach nor his son can please all the fans all the time.

SEAN THE PLAYER: Sam Alford's experiences with Steve would not be applicable to Sean.

"Steve was a star. Sean was a different kid," Coach Alford explains. Sean didn't start on the reserve team as a sophomore. As a junior he was the sixth man on the varsity, then became a starter and co-captain as a senior, and averaged almost 12 points a game.

Fans seemed to accept Sean Alford. New Castle went to the state finals when he was a junior and to the final game of the regional when he was a senior. He played well that year as a senior on a balanced-scoring team.

"We had two very good years and that helped immensely. The fans reacted well," Sam Alford explains.

THE PRESSURES INVOLVED: Sam Alford did not want to put more pressure on his sons than on other players, but he said, "I'm sure I probably did."

And he adds, "I didn't do a very good job with Sean. I wish I had that experience to do over again. I didn't realize how tough it had been on Sean to be Steve's little brother until it was too late."

He explains some people are cruel unintentionally. "Sometimes people would knock at the door of our house, Sean would answer and they would ask if Steve was there. If Steve wasn't home they would just turn around and walk away.

"Some would say things like, 'Your brother averaged 37, what are you averaging?'

"Those things happened and it was a tough situation for Sean, but he handled it very well," his father adds.

Like big brother Steve, Sean hung around the gym, but he might be playing on the ropes instead of shooting baskets. "Sean liked to have fun. He enjoyed life. He played cowboys and Indians, cops and robbers, kick-the-can. Steve didn't do a whole lot of that," Coach Alford recalls.

AN ENJOYABLE EXPERIENCE: Sam Alford's experiences may be of help to coaches who will have their sons as players in the future.

"I put a lot of burden on Steve's shoulders. I made him responsible for getting the team fired up. He was responsible for keeping the team in line, he was responsible for making sure everyone was ready to play. I expected him do an awful lot of things. I know that when you are seventeen there is a lot of life you would like to live without having to do all those things."

And he adds, "I probably made more demands of my two sons than I did of the other players. A lot of times coaches are afraid of that. Some coaches think they have to be very tough on their own sons. I think I was guilty of that."

An example: Steve had been on a roll, scoring in the forty-point range for three or four games, and the New Castle Trojans were ranked in the top five teams in the state. Naturally, Steve was getting all the ink in the papers. The team had accepted that, but Sam Alford knew human nature might take over, making some players envious.

That's why he told Steve at practice one day, "If I get mad at you today, you stand there and take it." Coach Alford waited about an hour for Steve to make some kind of mistake. He didn't. So, like Coach Bob Knight, he decided to test him on defense. "I started chewing on him and kicked him out of practice."

His intention was to prove his son would not be treated with favoritism, no matter how much he scored. "Things like that let the players know Steve wasn't above criticism," Sam Alford adds.

In reality, Steve Alford was yelled at quite regularly through the four years he was at New Castle and the four years he was at IU.

"He came out of it a pretty strong person," his dad concludes.

For six straight years, Sam Alford had his sons on his varsity teams, and "it was very, very enjoyable. I wish I had it to do over again," he admits, adding, "I know now I would relax a little more and not worry about what other people might think."

A coach can't always enjoy what his son does on the floor. He has to watch the entire team. "A lot of times, when we walked to the dressing room, an assistant coach would mention that Steve had scored in the forties. I couldn't have told you five baskets he'd made. I was so involved with the team, the team concept and what we were doing, that I couldn't enjoy watching my sons play until I went home and watched it on the VCR. And then I'd watch it as a father rather than as a coach."

STEVE'S STORY: Steve Alford can't remember a time when he didn't want to have a ball in his hands, "a racquet ball, a golf ball, a billiard ball, a baseball, a basketball. Ball was always at the end of it. I shot into a little sewing basket seven or eight inches in diameter. I did that when Mom was doing laundry, folding clothes, preparing supper. I was always throwing ping-pong balls into cans."

All that, he says, helped him with this touch and his eye-hand coordination.

As a first grader in Martinsville, Steve Alford went from Poston Road School to the high school gym, where he stayed until practice was over about 6:00 p.m. "I was around the game about four hours a day, just messing around—rebounding for someone, dribbling, shooting. I was a pest to a lot of those high school kids. I wanted to play one-on-one, I wanted to shoot 'Horse.'"

Steve Alford was on the bench during games. "I didn't always know what was going on during timeouts, but as a kid you pick up on things even if you are not comprehending it at the time. I was there during timeouts with ten seconds left and the game tied. I could feel the tension on the bench. I think those kinds of things come back to you later and you understand them."

In the beginning, it was difficult for Steve and Sam Alford to separate the father-son, coach-player relationship. Steve explains: "I was young, immature, still growing and developing not only as a player, but as a person. It was tough on me. It was tough on Dad because he had all the pressures of other parents, but he also had the pressure of having a son on the team. He had to deal with that. It was a lot easier on me as a player than for him as a coach.

"Once I got to be a sophomore and everyone knew I should be playing

BROTHERS AND DAD: Indiana star Steve Alford (left) had the experience of playing for his dad, New Castle Coach Sam Alford (above) and suiting up with his brother, Sean

it got easier on me as a player and him as a coach."

HEROES: As a youngster, Steve watched players like Magic Johnson and Larry Bird, but he didn't try to model himself after them. "I wanted to model my game after someone I might be like when I grew up."

Jerry Sichting, who played for Sam Alford at Martinsville, would be that model. "He was six-feet-one, 170-175 pounds, a good shooter, a hard worker, a good ball-handler and overall a good, smart player," Steve Alford explains.

"I tried to pick up those traits and do the things he was doing. He really set the tone as far as my attitude."

As a first, second, and third grader young Alford talked to Sichting often. But he admits, "I was only a kid. He was a star." (Sichting became an Indiana All-Star and played at Purdue and in the NBA).

That relationship may be why Steve Alford helped youngsters when he grew up and became a star himself.

Steve Alford, unlike his dad, doesn't feel he was under more pressure because he was the coach's son. He knows his dad was hard on him, but he adds, "There is a difference in being hard on someone and putting pressure on him. I don't think I had any pressure. I always felt I could average two points a game for Dad and he would still care for me and love me. He always treated me like I was his son.

"I never felt he was going to disown me if I didn't have a 30-point night. That was a joy and it made it much more comfortable for me to play for him."

Like Jerry Sichting, Steve Alford became a role model for youngsters throughout Indiana. He didn't notice the attention too much in high school, but he did after he went to Indiana and made the U.S. Olympic team after his freshman year.

After that, he explains, "It was tough to go to the malls, it was tough to go to McDonald's, and it was tough to do the routine things other students did. When you are thought of fairly highly you have to watch what you do."

That was a role that came fairly easy to Steve Alford. "I was brought up in a Christian home where we went to church and Sunday School. I started my faith very early and I think that makes it easy to keep things in perspective."

ADVICE TO OTHERS: Any young player, whether he plays for his father or some other coach, can learn from what Steve Alford has to say. "I think everyone is playing for his dad. I don't think it is just coaches' sons. Obviously, if a kid is playing for his dad who is the coach, he is going to have some pressure.

"He should be aware his dad is going to be a little harder on him, kick him out of practice, or sit him down and talk to him, not because he has done anything wrong, but just to prove he's not showing favoritism.

"I think that's what Dad did. He threw me out of practice seven or eight times in high school. Sometimes I wasn't doing anything wrong, sometimes I was. More times than not it was to show he wasn't getting complacent with me, that he wasn't showing favoritism.

"I played for Coach Bob Knight at Indiana, Coach John MacLeod at Dallas, Coach Don Nelson at San Francisco. And at all those places I always thought I was playing for my dad, too.

"Every kid would rather please his father than please his coach. So every kid is playing for his father."

A SPECIAL BOND: Steve Alford had dozens of great games at New Castle. But they don't stand out, he says. "They don't mean nearly as much to me as the three to five p.m. practices. We always came in on Saturday mornings for shoot-arounds. That meant more in a father-and-son relationship than going out and scoring 40 points. You get a lot of individual satisfaction from big scoring nights. But the most meaningful were those times we were together, whether it was just watching films together on Sundays or going scouting with him. Those were times I will really cherish."

Postscript: Sam Alford was looking forward to another successful year at New Castle during the 1989-90 season. Steve Alford expected to continue in the NBA and Sean Alford continued his studies at Indiana University.

Steve Alford hints he may be interested in coaching, preferably in college, in the years ahead. But if he goes into high school coaching and has a son, he would want to coach him.

"If I could give to my son half as much as my dad gave to me, my son would definitely be on the right track to succeed."

Indianapolis Star

SIBLINGS: Sean (front) at his brother Steve's 1987 wedding

Those Champion Seasons

BILL SHEPHERD AND SONS BILLY, DAVE, AND STEVE

FLASHBACK: It is 1945 and a small-town basketball star is making a big splash on the sports pages.

His name is Bill Shepherd, and his exploits have attracted the attention of sports writers and college coaches. He is named to the Indiana All-Star team, a prelude to his eventual enrollment at Butler University, where he will play for Tony Hinkle.

The years pass. Bill Shepherd performs well at Butler, graduates, and takes a coaching job at Mitchell, a southern Indiana school that has fallen on hard times since its 1940 team lost in the championship game of the state tournament.

A son, named Billy, is born, and two years later, David arrives.

A GENERATION LATER: Bill Shepherd has been coaching at Carmel for a decade after a successful career at Mitchell.

Little Billy Shepherd has grown up, played four years for his dad at Carmel, scored a total of 2,465 points, the third highest figure at that time for an Indiana school boy, and is named Mr. Basketball, 1968.

He is joined his senior year by brother David, a sophomore. Two years later, David finishes his high school career with 2,226 points, and helps take his dad's team to the final game of the 1970 state championship. He, too, is named Mr. Basketball.

Bill Shepherd then steps down as basketball coach at Carmel to devote full time as athletic director. Daughter Cindy is in high school by then. Girls' basketball hasn't become a big sport yet in high schools. But she is at the games, cheering, until she graduates in 1972.

Time passes. It is now 1977 and a third son, Steve, is a sophomore on a senior-laden Carmel team, which wins the state basketball championship. He doesn't have a big role on that team but he does flash a state-championship ring, something his brothers don't have.

Steve will play two more years at Carmel.

THE PRESENT: A third generation of Shepherds is growing up. Scott, son of Billy, grandson of Bill, becomes a starter as a freshman on Carmel's 1988-89 team. He is one of fourteen grandchildren, seven boys and seven girls, of Bill and Edie Shepherd. Most, if not all, suffer with incurable cases of basketball fever.

The legend grows.

BILLY AND DAVID AS PLAYERS: Billy Shepherd became a mascot for the Mitchell team when he was about three, sometimes shooting and dribbling between halves.

All the Shepherd boys were always around the gym. Bill Shepherd never had to force them to play. When his teams took a break from practice, or he was speaking to his players, his sons were out on the floor shooting.

When Steve grew older, all three were usually found at the gym shooting. That helped them become better players. "Like anything else," Bill Shepherd explains, "the more practice you get the better you can develop your skills."

Billy Shepherd adds that he spent so much time in the gym he thinks he may have been "a pain in the neck for the student managers."

The Shepherd boys sat on the bench with the team and went scouting with their father, who adds, "Anytime we went anywhere they were there. They just wanted to be part of it."

All three boys were interested in basketball—they watched, they listened, and they learned. For example, Billy elaborates, "Passing is so underrated in the game of basketball. Being around the game all the time when I was growing up helped my passing and ball-handling more than any other aspect of my game."

Bill Shepherd knows his sons were lucky to have opportunities, "But [to succeed] you have to want to develop those opportunities. You have to want to excel." His sons wanted to excel.

When the Shepherd boys were growing up, there were few basketball camps available. They sometimes gave demonstrations at summer camps, but Bill Shepherd adds, "I don't think either Billy or David ever attended an organized basketball camp.

"We weren't a rich family and back then $50-70 was a lot of money to us. They had access to the gym and we just felt we could give them a lot of training there."

Bill Shepherd didn't ponder long over whether to start Billy when he was a freshman. "He wasn't very tall or very big [125-130 pounds], but he had a lot of finesse and he had the ability to play. He was playing in front of three seniors and a junior, so he had to prove he could play."

Billy Shepherd recalls that was a rather difficult time for him: "Dad had to cut two seniors who had been on the team as juniors, so I started off with a couple of strikes against me. It is tough enough to play as a freshman, regardless of whether your dad is coach."

It didn't help, he adds, when he kicked the ball off his leg the first time he had it, then threw it out of bounds the second time he touched it. "It wasn't a great start," he admits. But things improved, and he ended up scoring 13 points in his varsity debut.

He felt relieved five or six games later, when a Tipton player stepped across his back and the upperclassmen came to his defense in a brief scuffle. It made him feel he had been accepted. He scored 24 points in that game, his season high.

The team won fifteen games. "It was a good start," Bill Shepherd adds.

When Billy was a sophomore, the team struggled to a .500 season after losing almost everyone else from the year before. "He was almost carrying us by himself," his dad says.

That so-so season had a happy ending. Billy hit the bucket that allowed Carmel to beat Noblesville and win its first sectional in forty-one years. "You would have thought we won the state tournament. I think Billy made a lot of friends that night," his dad smiles.

As might be expected, there were some complaints about Billy being the coach's son. "Some of those came from fans who didn't recognize his tremendous ball-handling and passing ability," his dad acknowledges, adding:

"There are a lot of players who can score, but not a lot of people who can make the big plays and give a teammate the ball at the right time. Those were things Billy was very, very good at."

From the time he started playing, Billy was almost like a coach on the floor. "If we were ahead," has dad recalls, "we knew he could take care of the basketball, go to the free-throw line, and hit his free throws."

By the time Dave was a freshman, the Carmel-Clay School Board had decided only sophomores, juniors, and seniors could play on the high school team.

Dave had the ability, his dad knew, but he would have to wait a year to join Billy on the varsity, which meant they would have only one year together.

Billy jokes that David's major role as a newcomer to the team was to get him the ball. If that was the case, Dave still got his share of the shots.

Bill Shepherd says David wasn't the great finesse player that Billy was, "but he would fight you down to the end. He was a great shooter and a great competitor." With the two Shepherds in the lineup, Carmel lost but three games in the 1967-68 season. The team won the sectional, but David and another player became sick before the regional and the team lost to Marion, 68-67.

"It was one of the most disappointing losses, I think, in my coaching career," Bill Shepherd adds.

David Shepherd still holds the state one-year scoring record (1,079 points) set in 1970. Only he, Steve Alford (1,078 points in 1983), and George

McGinnis (1,019 points in 1969) had scored more than 1,000 points in a single season as of 1989.

As a senior, David helped lead his dad's team to the final game of the 1970 state tournament, where Carmel lost to East Chicago Roosevelt, 76-62.

Dave Shepherd scored 88 points in two regional games at Anderson, then added 125 in the two semistate and state-final games.

Bill Shepherd was no longer coaching when Steve, his youngest son, reached high school. He thinks Steve has always felt bad about that. Steve says, "There are definite advantages of playing for your father. There also is lot of pressure. But I would have liked to have played for my father. I think he was an excellent coach."

"I had a tendency to look over my shoulder when I did something wrong, but it was more of a confidence factor. When Billy or David made an error, they didn't have to worry about whether they were going to be taken out of the game."

His dad adds, "If I had it to do over again I might have stayed in coaching

Indianapolis News

THE SHEPHERDS OF CARMEL: Dad Bill (center) with sons David and Billy—both named Mr. Basketball in high school

until he [Steve] got out of school. But he was a fine player and a fine son."

Even though Steve Shepherd didn't play for his father, he still felt pressure. "He was still the athletic director, still associated with the school. And when you are on a state championship team as a sophomore, people point fingers. There was a lot of jealousy. It didn't bother me on the road. It bothered me at home.

"I would hear things like, 'Your dad is the athletic director. That's why you are playing.' "I felt that pressure and I felt the pressure of following in Billy and David's footsteps."

WHAT HANDICAP? Billy Shepherd stepped in a hole on his paper route one Tuesday morning during the 1966-67 season. He awoke his dad and said, "I think I've broken my wrist."

A check showed the wrist was badly sprained, not broken, but it was a major concern to Bill Shepherd. Fort Wayne South, ranked No. 1 and featuring Mr. Basketball-to-be Willie Long, was due in Carmel for a game that Friday night.

The sprain didn't keep Billy Shepherd out of the game. He played left-handed, even shooting his free throws left handed, and scored 24 points. Carmel lost the game, but Bill Shepherd calls the performance "one of the most incredible exhibitions I have ever seen."

After that Billy Shepherd faced a lot of boxes-and-ones, triangles-and-twos, and junk defenses. When the defenses stopped him from scoring, he could still get the ball to someone who could.

A DIFFERENT PERSPECTIVE: Bill Shepherd knows what it is like for a coach to have sons as players. And he knows what it is to sit in the stands and watch a son play for another coach.

"You don't really know what goes on in the stands until you quit coaching. After twenty-one or twenty-two years I was back in the stands and I heard things I didn't hear as a coach. Or, maybe, you can close yours ears a little when you coach."

ANECDOTE: Carmel was at Muncie South for a game when Billy Shepherd was playing. The South players were making contact, bumping Billy, or so Coach Shepherd thought. "They were all over him," he recalls.

He admits he complained like every other coach when he didn't think the calls were right. At halftime, Shepherd confronted one of the referees and said, "They are all over Billy and you guys aren't calling them for fouls."

The referee, without batting an eye, feigned ignorance and replied, "Billy who?"

Bill Shepherd doesn't remember the referee, but he hasn't forgotten the incident or the humor in the referee's retort.

NO SPECIAL FAVORS: It is important, Bill Shepherd insists, to treat your sons like all other players. "There were times when I got on them in practice if they were loafing or we thought they weren't doing the job. You only do that because you do it to all the others. You certainly wouldn't do that to other players and not your sons."

He had to get on his sons in practice at times. "If you didn't get on players at times, you wouldn't be a good coach," he adds.

Billy recalls one incident when his dad disciplined him in no uncertain terms. "A junior, who had guarded me in practice for two years, was getting extremely physical one day in practice.

"We were working against the box-and-one and other defenses. After two years you get tired of someone holding, pushing and shoving you. I was dribbling the ball and I knew my antagonist would take the charge. I hit him pretty hard, but I wasn't trying to hurt him. I just wanted to get him off of me."

Coach Bill Shepherd stopped practice and let Billy know he didn't like what he had done and complained that he couldn't understand why Billy would do that to a teammate. He kicked Billy off the floor and didn't let him return during that practice session.

Looking back, Billy admits, "It taught me a lesson. The kid I ran over was the ninth or tenth man on the team, and Dad treated him just like he would any other player."

A GREAT EXPERIENCE: Bill Shepherd, looking back on coaching his sons: "It was a great experience. Teaching and coaching don't pay a lot even today. But I wouldn't change what I've done in my lifetime as a coach and athletic director.

"I still enjoy athletics. That's why I'm still athletic director. I never had any desire to be a principal. I've always wanted to stay close to athletics."

Postscript: Billy Shepherd also played at Butler and later in the old American Basketball Association. David played at Indiana and Mississippi and Steve at Indiana Central (now University of Indianapolis).

The Shepherds, from Grandma and Grandpa down to the youngest grandchildren, can often be seen at big games involving Indiana high school teams.

Bill remains as athletic director at Carmel. His three sons are now businessmen, but each is involved in coaching. David, aided by Steve, has coached the Carmel Pups' sixth-grade teams for years. Billy has had a lot of success as an AAU coach and his teams have won a number of championships.

Together Again

COACH BOB HEADY AND SON SCOTT

Turn back the calendar to 1981. Bob Heady is the coach at Shenandoah. His son Scott is one of the players who leads his team to the Final Four of the Indiana state tournament.

Flip the calendar forward. It is 1989 and Coach Bob Heady is head coach at Carmel High School where his son Scott coaches the junior varsity.

Together again, father and son.

* * *

Scott Heady had graduated from the University of Indianapolis and taken a teaching job, expecting to wait a year or two for a coaching vacancy, but when two assistant coaches left, he chose to take the "B" team job rather than become a varsity assistant. "I wanted a team of my own," he admits.

It was only natural Scott Heady would want to coach. He had been around basketball from the time he was born. "Every time I made a coaching change," his father, Bob, relates, "we tried very hard to locate close enough so Scott would be able to walk to the gym and be there at practice. As soon as he could walk and bounce a ball he was around the gym."

He absorbed like osmosis what he observed; he applied it by spending hours in gymnasiums. "If I had work to do at school on weekends," his dad adds, "he would spend all day in the gym if I allowed him to."

Scott sat on the bench with his dad until he was in junior high. "I listened in on every huddle, every locker-room discussion. I think I learned more there than anywhere."

He picked idols, role models, on his dad's teams. Most often, they were players who hustled and worked hard, not always the super players.

Scott participated in his dad's summer camps and recalls winning contests against junior-high kids when he was in the second and third grades. "I was more advanced than they were because I had been around the gym so much. I would win some contests, then get mad because my dad wouldn't give me the awards."

Bob Heady knew his son might be a better-than-average player when he was still in grade school. He could dribble with either hand and had developed good shooting skills. But Heady, the father, made it a point not to interfere with coaches who had his son on teams through junior high school.

"If he was taken out of the game, his coach did it and I never got involved. If Scott asked about how he could do something better, I would help him with that."

Coach Heady took the Shenandoah job before Scott entered the eighth grade. He calls it "probably the best move I have made during my coaching career."

Scott Heady joined a class of other good players who took their basketball as seriously as he did. As eighth graders, their team finished the season with a 15-0 record. They promised greatness.

Scott played on the JV team as a freshman. His dad was determined not to show any favoritism. "Scott had the ability and the skills, but I thought there might be too much pressure for him, even though he would have handled it."

In hindsight, he admits, "That probably was one of the biggest mistakes I made in coaching. If I had it to do over again, I wouldn't do it. I would put him on the varsity in a heartbeat."

Scott still got some valuable experience on the JV team composed of other good players and was challenged in practices and in games. And it didn't delay his development.

Scott, himself, has no second thoughts: "I was five-feet-nine and weighed 120 pounds. I'm sure I wasn't ready for the varsity and that's one of the reasons I didn't play. I think playing on the JV team probably helped me more than playing on the varsity would have. I just don't think I was physically ready to play."

He moved into the starting lineup as a sophomore on a team that continued to get better for the next two years.

Coach Heady gave his son a lot of responsibility, and he expected a lot from him as point guard. Scott was expected to hit ninety percent of his free throws, although other players were expected to hit seventy percent. He was expected to play flawlessly and to score in double figures.

By the time Scott Heady was a senior, the team had jelled into a cohesive unit. Shenandoah won the Indianapolis semistate before losing in the afternoon game of the state finals to Vincennes, the eventual state champion.

COACH-PLAYER, FATHER-SON: Bob Heady didn't hesitate to criticize his son, the player. "If he needed to have a good chewing out, I would get after him. And I would praise him as much, but no more, than I would anyone else."

There were, however, situations where Bob Heady was both a coach and a father and it was difficult to separate the two.

For example: "If he missed a free throw or missed a basket in a key

A COMMON GOAL IN SIGHT: Bob Heady (left), who coached, and now coaches with, his son Scott

situation, it bothered me not only as a coach, but as a father. It was probably a double hurt.

"Those things happen. Everyone wants his son or daughter to be the best he or she can be. You want them to do well and if they don't there is some pain. If you are coaching him or her those things happen."

Growing up as the son of a coach, Scott Heady knew he had to be better, that he had to work harder than anyone else if he wanted to play.

He knew he would have to earn whatever role he was given as a player. And he didn't expect any more, or any less, than any other kid who came out for the team.

It was the same at school, where his dad was a teacher.

Bob Heady recalls one incident when he showed some emotion for his son as a player. "When the 1981 tournament was over and we had been eliminated by Vincennes, I felt some pain.

"It was over as far as me being his coach. From then on, I would see him play as a father and as a fan. It hurt to know I couldn't coach him any more or that I no longer could depend on his ability to help me be a good coach."

Other than that, the Headys had no trouble separating the father-son, coach-player role.

Scott never complained or used the fact his father was coach for special treatment. Bob Heady adds, "When I took him out of the game, he'd never give me any back-talk or any mean looks. He'd go to the bench and sit down. Luckily I didn't have to take him out of the game very often."

SOME ADVICE: Now that he is a coach himself, Scott Heady can offer advice to sons of coaches from two perspectives.

He knows that the son of a coach has to push himself a little harder. "It's a family-type thing. You have more interest in the team because it's your father for whom you are playing."

A father expects more out of his son and the son may put pressure on himself. He wants to prove he can play, he doesn't want to make his father look bad. "That is always in the back of your mind," he adds.

"My dad couldn't stand there in practice and preach to other kids if I wasn't going to do what I was told."

And, he knows, a coach's son sometimes feels like the preacher's kid. "Everybody is always watching you. Even the team. Some people are just waiting for you to mess up."

Despite all that, he concludes, "Just remember there will be more good than bad. Don't let all those extra things bother you. Don't let the pressure get to you. Know that you are going to succeed because of all the hours in the gym. Just go out and be yourself."

A REPEAT PERFORMANCE? Bob Heady enjoyed the years as a player. "I wish I could start all over again. I wish I could start him as a freshman again and repeat the whole experience. Those were some of my best years in coaching."

And Scott would do it over again, too, and adds: "I think the success we had when we went to the state finals may not have been so much because of talents but because we were a team. I think I knew what Dad wanted done and I was kind of like a mediator between him and the team. We had played a lot in the summer. When I asked the other players to work toward our senior season they reacted like, 'It's the coach's son asking me to play. I can't say no.'"

Postscript: In a way, Scott Heady is proving himself all over again as a coach on his father's staff. He eventually wants to be a varsity coach, but is willing to wait for the right time and the right place.

The Bashers in Wabash

COACH RON SLATON AND SON MARC

Chances are neither Ron, Linda, nor Marc Slaton will ever forget the city of Wabash.

They will remember, the good and the bad.

It was there Ron Slaton taught and coached for four years. It was there Marc played four years of high school basketball, where he scored 1,575 points, where he graduated as salutatorian of his class.

It was there where Marc was in the Honor Society and vice president of his class.

It was there where a teacher in class, a day after Marc had scored 27 points in a game, asked a question, looked at Marc and said, "We'll let the ball-hog answer that."

It was there all three Slatons felt the jealousy and envy with which a few people in communities sometimes greet newcomers . . . and basketball players who might replace native sons.

It would take a long time for Marc Slaton to be accepted by fans and students.

Ron Slaton had some hesitation about starting his son as a freshman in the 1985-86 season. There were some seniors on the team, but only one who had started. And, Coach Slaton says, "Some of those kids just weren't good enough to play.

"Marc, even though he was just a freshman, was so much more skilled and so much better at ball-handling. He could do things they couldn't do."

Coach Slaton tried to downplay Marc's role as a freshman. "He should have been the point guard as a freshman, but I used him at off guard so he wouldn't be handling the ball as much. And I tried to play down Marc's role and give the other kids as much mention in the newspaper as I could."

"It was a tough situation for him. And I know it was tough for the other kids. In Indiana, you have to go home and listen to Mom and Dad," he adds.

As a freshman, Marc Slaton suffered indignities at the hands of some of his own teammates. They poured urine from a bottle on him in the showers. At games, he heard assorted language and was taunted by jealous students, mostly upperclassmen.

Marc withstood the barrage and finished the season with an 8-point-per-game average and a total of 98 assists.

Still, the community resentment continued. Ron Slaton remembers the meeting he had for parents before Marc's sophomore season:

"My wife had always [ridden] on the team bus to away games and it was never mentioned. Now that Marc was playing on the varsity, it suddenly became a problem. She was Marc's mommy, or so the other parents said." They contended she was not only the coach's wife, but the mother of a player.

Ron Slaton had the last word. "She is my wife, no matter what. She will ride the bus and the only thing you can do is go to the school board and have my job."

That, he emphasized, is the way things have to be in coaching. Some coaches *do* let their wives ride with friends to games. "That," he adds, "might be the reason the friends' sons get to play basketball. It doesn't matter which way you go, you're going to get some criticism."

There was still more abuse. Wabash fans, possibly with an assist by some cheerleaders, once booed Marc. Three cheerleaders later came to Linda Slaton and apologized.

On another occasion, Marc was injured and his mother exclaims, "Honest to God, I thought he was dead. Ron went out on the floor, like he would for any of his players." Linda Slaton says she didn't hear it, but an assistant coach's wife told her later that one lady, who caused a lot of problems, had yelled, "Oh, Daddy is going out to see about Sonny."

She then shouted to Mrs. Slaton, "Sit down, lady. I can't see what's going on down there."

Linda Slaton adds, "Some people at Wabash were super, but there were always a few who caused problems."

It is not unusual, Coach Slaton insists, for fans to be harder on the team's best players. They may do that, he explains, because their own sons aren't that good.

"That's the way it has been every place we have been. The best player has always taken abuse. No game is ever good enough," Mrs. Slaton explains.

Marc Slaton scored 50 points in a game as a junior. "After that," his mother adds, "nothing else was good enough for some fans. If Marc scored 30, it was, like, big deal, so what?' The talk around town would be, 'Slaton only got 30 last night.'"

MARC AS A PLAYER: Marc Slaton stepped up his scoring to 14.8 points a game and averaged 6.2 assists a game as a sophomore. He followed that up with a 28-point average as a junior, when he had 4.8 assists per game.

His scoring average dipped slightly (to 25.9 points a game) as a senior when he was moved to forward to give the team more rebounding even though he is just 6'1". "It was a sacrifice for him," his dad contends, "because he should have been a point or shooting guard. Unfortunately he didn't have that luxury."

That jealousy hurt, Marc Slaton admits. "But it made me grow more as a person." He began to feel he was being accepted by his teammates during his junior year. "We had one senior and the rest were juniors and sophomores. We really got along well."

He agrees his freshman and sophomore years were "really tough," explaining, "it is human nature to want to be accepted. Knowing I really wasn't accepted kind of hurt, but when I came home each night my dad would explain to me why that was. He said other players wanted to be as good as I was so they felt I might be getting special treatment, which I wasn't."

Marc Slaton says he felt a lot of pressure as a sophomore and that it continued to build when he was a junior. "It got to the point I would be dry-heaving in the locker room before a game.

"I remember right before my 50-point game [in the Wabash County] tourney. I was on the locker-room floor and I just couldn't get up. Then I went out and had a game like that . . . so I thought I should be that way before every game," he recalled, laughing.

As a senior, he says he forced himself to relax. "I told myself to remember that it is just a game. I went out and had fun and didn't get nervous."

PLAYER-COACH, FATHER-SON: Ron Slaton stressed to his son that he was the coach at the gym, the father at home.

"When I come home, I'll tell you your coach is stupid. Every other parent would tell his son that. But you have to realize when we go back to the gym tomorrow, I'll be just as stupid as I was tonight."

MOMENT OF GLORY: Marc Slaton and father/coach Ron Slaton (left inset)—Marc cuts twine after scoring 50 points in a tournament game

And Coach Slaton realizes he was harder on his son than on other players. By the time Marc was a junior, his teammates were beginning to realize he was getting no favors from his dad. They were asking him, "Why is he on you? You didn't do anything wrong."

That, Coach Slaton believes, probably helped Marc in the end. "He was accepted because I was on him more."

Being harder on your best player isn't unusual, he adds. "I did that with other players who weren't my son. You do it with players from whom you expect a lot. You let up on players who aren't quite as good. Maybe you shouldn't."

Marc recalls one night in practice when his shooting was bad. "The ball wasn't going down and I got frustrated and started lollygagging around. Dad saw that and he told me, 'Just get outta here.'"

On another occasion Marc was coming down the floor and "a defensive player stepped out in front of me. I spun around and did a 360 and shot the ball. I probably missed it, but I don't recall." The move didn't impress Coach Slaton. "We don't need that," he told his son, and kicked him out of practice.

Marc adds, "I tried to explain to him that was the only option except to run the guy over, but I guess he didn't think he needed an explanation."

A RULE IS A RULE: Marc Slaton always wanted to play basketball. His interest may have been whetted when as a toddler he tossed a ball into a paper sack on the door in the Slaton house.

"He was always into about every kind of sport there was when he was small," says his father, who earned fourteen letters in athletics himself at Tunnelton High School.

Like many sons of coaches, Marc went to the gym as a toddler. He played at the Frankfort Boys Club as a six-year-old when his dad was coaching at Clinton Central.

Marc Slaton was in the second or third grade when he learned what it was like to be yelled at by his dad, the coach.

Ron Slaton had told Marc he couldn't shoot beyond the free-throw line. Some of the Clinton Central players egged him into going further and further out on the court.

"He fired one up from out there and I ran him out of the gym. He ran into a classroom and got under a desk where his mother found him. She was pretty upset about it," his dad recalls.

Marc Slaton recovered from that incident and diagrammed his first play. He gave it to his dad, then asked him if he had used it.

Marc continued to play organized ball up through the grades. As a fourth grader, he was on the Muncie Boys Club team when his dad coached at Cowan. Some of his teammates on that team later played for Muncie Central when the Bearcats won the state championship in 1988.

Marc played about ninety games as a sixth grader, counting those at the Boys Club and school.

He often went scouting with his father. "I picked up a lot from that," Marc recalls. "I was very observant when I went to games. I didn't run around like a little fire engine. I watched and tried to learn as much as I could."

Marc Slaton played in the seventh grade at North Knox near Vincennes and in the eighth grade at Greenfield. By then it was obvious Marc Slaton was an outstanding shooter.

His first game as a seventh grader was an example. North Knox played Loogootee, whose coach had seen Marc Slaton play in the summer. The coach used a box-and-one to defense young Slaton.

HIGHLIGHTS: For Marc, winning the Wabash County championship when he was a junior was his biggest thrill. It wasn't because he scored 50 points in the championship game. It was because he had helped underdog Wabash win the title for his dad.

For his dad, "The biggest thrill was when another coach asked Marc to appear at his clinic. It was good to know one of your peers thought he was the kind of kid he wanted to speak to his players.

"A woman teacher next door told me she hopes her son grows up like Marc. Another teacher named her son after him. When someone comes up and says your kid has class, it makes you feel that things went right."

Linda Slaton says, "I just loved watching [Marc] play. The county tourney was my biggest thrill. It was great."

. . . AND LOWLIGHTS: It is difficult for a high scorer like Marc Slaton to maintain a low profile, no matter how hard he may try. Marc once refused to go to a school function after the big county tourney. His parents had bought the ticket long before, but Marc insisted other students might think the only reason he was there was because he had scored 50 points in a game and wanted to be seen.

Linda Slaton explains, "He doesn't want people to think he is better than they are. Some ballplayers who get a little ink sometimes are ruined by the attention."

The teacher who had referred to Marc Slaton as a ball-hog later apologized to him in private, saying he was only teasing.

Marc Slaton replied, "An awful lot of people say things to me who are not teasing. So how am I supposed to know the difference?"

AN ENCORE: Would Ron Slaton want to coach his son again? He replies: "Oh, I would! There wouldn't be any hesitation. And I would even do it over again with this group we had here this last season. We had a lot of problems and a lot of things we had to battle through the year, but the year was fun."

And he adds, "Marc has turned out to be a well-rounded person. I think most coaches' kids do."

Postscript: Marc Slaton is attending the University of South Carolina-Spartanburg, a Division II school, on a full athletic scholarship. He plans to study pre-med and eventually plans to pursue a career in sports medicine. Ron and Linda Slaton moved to Rock Hill, South Carolina, in the summer of 1989. That put them close enough to Spartanburg to see Marc play at the college level.

Something To Value

COACH PHIL WADDELL AND SON MATT WADDELL

It took just one season as a spectator to convince Phil Waddell he should return to coaching as a profession.

Waddell had been head coach at Centerville when son Matt was younger, but had quit to operate the family grocery business back home in Russiaville.

He didn't get completely away from basketball, however. He was a volunteer coach when Matt was in the sixth, seventh, and eighth grades, but had no role during his freshman year.

That was when he decided he missed basketball and wanted to resume his career as a coach.

As a freshman, Matt was on the varsity at Western High School, the first guard off the bench for Coach Tom Lewis. Phil Waddell had no complaints about how his son was treated. "Tom brought Matt along well," he explains.

Although Waddell wanted to return to basketball, he didn't want to be a head coach. "I felt I would be more comfortable as an assistant where I didn't have to make the final decisions on Matt."

Unfortunately there was no job at Western that interested him. He considered a few options around central Indiana, and decided to become assistant coach for Larry Angle at Tipton. Waddell and Angle spent hours talking basketball philosophy and determining how their responsibilities would be divided.

"We [members of the Waddell family] were looking for a school with a coach who had a good basketball background. We thought Tipton was a good place." The Waddells, Phil, wife Jane, daughter Monica, and son Matt, moved to Tipton in the summer of 1987. Two years later, Phil Waddell was satisfied the situation had been good for him and his family, and for the community of Tipton.

"I have been allowed to be as involved as I wanted to be," Phil Waddell adds. "I like to do the organizational and motivational things. Larry's strengths are in the coaching and what goes on between the black lines."

And he insists, "Coach Angle is making the final decisions and he is calling the shots."

It was a winning combination. The Tipton team finished the 1988-89 season with a 22-4 record and didn't lose in the state tournament until the semistate.

MATT WADDELL THE PLAYER: When he was growing up, Matt Waddell spent time in the gym and watched his dad conduct his camps at Southmont and Centerville. He absorbed a lot of the fundamentals that were being taught and he played against older kids, which helped him improve more quickly.

As a first grader, he played in a biddy-ball program at Crawfordsville with youngsters his age in the morning, then went to his dad's camp in the afternoon to compete against older players.

He continued to play up through the grades, then was on his dad's teams in the sixth, seventh, and eighth grades in the Western school system at Russiaville. Matt Waddell always tried to make the game fun for his son. "If it comes to a point where it isn't fun for either one of us, it'll be time to look for something else to do.

"If Matt wants to work on basketball, I am going to be there to help him. He has been around the game enough and watched enough tapes and enough other games to know what he has to work on."

Phil Waddell hasn't pushed his son. "I feel it has to come from him. He has to want to improve. That's not to say that we don't ask him whether he is working on certain things. We're still prodding him along a little, but I think it has to be self-motivated.

"It has to be his goals he wants to accomplish, not mine."

In the summer between his junior and senior years, Matt Waddell had a Monday, Wednesday, and Friday routine in which he arose at 5:00 a.m., went to the gym, and shot 200 jump shots and 100 free throws and lifted weights each day. He played basketball in the gym on Tuesdays and Thursdays when he wasn't playing on the Municipal Gardens AAU team out of Indianapolis with Eric Montross of state-champion Lawrence North, Damon

Bailey of Bedford-North Lawrence, and other seventeen-year-old standouts from across the state.

Matt started on the Tipton varsity as a sophomore, filling one of the guard positions that had been vacated by graduation.

Gene Milner's 1989 Indiana High School Basketball Record Book named Matt Waddell as the most complete player in Indiana during the 1988-89 season. He qualified for every category—scoring (22.1 points per game), field goal (66%), three-point (53%) and free-throw (80%) percentages, rebounding (6.7 average), assists (9.1) average, and steals (4.6) averages.

"Matt prides himself in being a complete player, not just a shooter," his father says. "He wants to excel and he works hard in all areas. We had to urge him to be a little more offensive minded and to shoot the ball more."

Phil Waddell had worked with his son so long, they only needed two or three key words to communicate during games.

"If his shot was off, I could give him a sign from the bench about what he was doing wrong. A father-son relationship makes communication a lot easier from the bench to floor," Coach Waddell explains.

"It's like having another coach on the floor. He can communicate to the other players what the coaches want done and it saves timeouts."

Matt Waddell says his son leads by example. His work ethic is good, his mannerisms are the same whether his team is up by twenty points or down by twenty points or whether he hasn't hit a shot, or he has hit all of them.

"He is not a yeller or a screamer, but he is in control of a game, whether it is the first possession of the game or whether he has the ball with two seconds to go."

As the son of a coach, Matt Waddell learned that it is just as important to get the ball to the right person as it is to score the basket.

PRIZED POSSESSIONS: Phil Waddell and Larry Angle treat Matt Waddell like other players. Coach Waddell explains: "Parents of players have given us their most prized possession, their sons, to work with. Coach Angle and I feel it is an honor for them to allow their sons to be in our program.

"We feel our job is not only to check the scoreboard on Friday and Saturday nights, but to evaluate what morals and values we have taught the team during the week.

"If a team leaves at the end of the season and the only thing it remembers is that it was 22-4, then the coach and I haven't had a good year.

"The players need to remember lessons they learned along the way about hard work, lessons about coming back the night after a loss and and giving it your best effort.

"If that happens, our season also has been a success. That is our number-one priority."

And he adds, "The first thing you have to look at when you take a coaching position is the responsibility you have to the individual player. You need to consider how you can help those individuals grow, not only as basketball players, but as young men."

MATT WADDELL ONE-ON-ONE: Matt Waddell knows why he spends an average of four hours a day in the gym. "Every day you miss puts you a day behind the other kids who are working."

When he plays in the Tipton gym on summer nights, he decides in

"It's like having another coach on the floor."
—Tipton Coach Phil Waddell on son Matt

advance which part of his game he wants to emphasize. One night it might be ball-handling, the next night defense.

Matt enjoyed playing for his dad at Western. "He pushed me harder than anyone else and I needed it. He knew when I was loafing. All the other coaches before that would let me get away with that, I guess, because I was a little ahead of everyone else. They would let me slide and he wouldn't let me do that."

Matt missed his father's coaching as a freshman. "He didn't say anything when he was sitting in the stands, but he might tell me some things later. He set goals for me each game—so many rebounds, so many assists.

"As far as coaching, he couldn't do anything, which was a kind of disadvantage for me because I was used to having him on the sidelines."

Being a complete player comes somewhat naturally for a coach's son. "Being a point guard, you know how important assists are, that they are as important, or even more so, than points. I'm six-feet-three playing against smaller guards, so I should be able to get a lot of rebounds."

As the son of a coach, he was used to moving. "We had a good team in my grade at Western. I hated leaving those guys because I knew we'd be good in a couple of years, but I knew Dad wanted to get back into coaching. I knew he enjoyed it and I wanted him to be one of my coaches the last three years [of school]."

The fact he was quickly accepted at Tipton by other players and Coach Angle made the transition easier. When Tipton played at Western later, Matt Waddell heard a lot of screaming, which he accepted. "That's part of it, I guess." His former teammates, however, understood. "They were good about it."

Matt likes the arrangement at Tipton. "Dad and Coach Angle work well together. They know each other's strong points and weaknesses."

And he knows he often will be the first player criticized. "They get on me if I do something wrong. If another player did the same thing, they wouldn't say as much, maybe not anything at all. If I make a mental mistake, they make sure I realize I've done something wrong. They might not say anything to another player who might not know the game as well as I do."

Fans also let Matt know when he has a bad game, probably because they have grown to expect superior performances.

The lines between father-son and player-coach are clear-cut for Matt Waddell. "When we walk into the gym, he's the coach and I'm the player. When we leave the gym, he's the father and I'm his son.

"When I step on the floor, I respect him as my coach."

A coach's son, he adds, has to work a little harder. "He has to go out and out-hustle the other guys. If he doesn't, his dad will be on him because he wants the best for his son. And that's a positive point, because the harder you work the farther you are going to get."

Postscript: Matt Waddell had a 3.3 grade index going into his senior year and had a good background in mathematics which he planned to use in a professional career. But, first, he looked forward to playing basketball for a Division I school.

Double-Teamed

COACH JIM MATTHEWS AND SONS JAMIE AND SCOTT

Jim Matthews laughed as he looked forward to the 1989-90 season at New Washington.

"I'm not going to be nearly as smart. I'm going to miss the twins, no doubt about it."

The twins were Scott and Jamie, his sons, who had made life on the basketball courts of southern Indiana enjoyable for their father the previous four years.

"It was a great experience," Jim Matthews explains. "They allowed me to accomplish things in coaching I had never accomplished before. We won two sectionals, played in the Indiana Hall of Fame games, and I was invited to speak at several clinics. They provided me the success on the court that permitted me to receive a certain amount of recognition in coaching."

The 5'10" Matthews twins combined to give their father one of the best guard tandems in the state. They, talented center Shannon Arthur, and some role-players helped New Washington record a 66-8 mark over three seasons.

LEARNING THE GAME: Jim and Sugie Matthews bought each of the twins a biddy basketball when they were six months old.

"They were raised in a basketball environment," Coach Matthews adds. Their mother, who had been a physical education teacher, started taking them to practice almost as soon as they could walk.

Jim Matthews kept a basketball goal at a level the twins could reach until they were four years old. By then they were shooting at a regulation goal and scoring with regularity. "They didn't do it underhand, they actually shot the ball," Jim Matthews explains, pointing to a picture of Scott firing left-handed.

As second graders, the twins played on a fifth-grade team that went unbeaten. The teams they played on won the Greater Clark County championship the next three years. And their eighth-grade team finished the season 19-3 and won a tournament among much larger schools.

The boys developed their own work habits and their dad gave them a list of ball-handling and footwork drills which they posted on the wall of their room. Each day they worked on the things their dad had asked them to do.

Unlike some coaches, Jim Matthews believes a youngster has to learn to shoot on his own, then be given drills to fit what he does naturally. "Jamie and Scott shot the ball completely different, but in ways that were most efficient for each of them," he explains.

It is difficult to argue with his reasoning. Scott averaged 17.4 points as a junior and 18.7 as a senior, Jamie 20.4 as a junior and 18.3 as a senior. Both were among the state leaders in assists.

Jim Matthews made sure his sons were exposed to athletics, whether it was basketball, baseball, or other sports. But he insists they weren't pushed into playing. They developed that interest on their own.

"We made sure they saw the best people in their field. When they were in elementary school, for example, we took them to see Larry Schellenberg, who played for Floyd Central High School [and was a 1981 Indiana All-Star]. I thought he was one of the best high school players I ever saw at handling the ball and helping his teammates be better. I didn't want Jamie or Scott to copy him, but I wanted them to understand that was how the game was to be played. I wanted them to know that the object was to win and that you did that by making your teammates better."

The twins did not have great physical characteristics, but they offset that with good hand-eye coordination and court awareness. They learned how to maximize their knowledge of the game, when to pass, when to shoot, when to hit the open man. As their father explains, "They were gifted with the ability to perceive how things were done and the ability to carry them out."

Scott and Jamie Matthews averaged about three hours a day in the gym, year-around. They realized they had to work harder because of their lack of size.

They often were joined in the gym by four assistant coaches, Phil Johnson, Brian McEwen, Brad Bastain, and Jeff Rhoten. They worked out as friends, not as coaches, the twins explain.

Jim Matthews says his sons' work ethics are "tremendous." "Their feet have callouses you wouldn't believe. Their toes are almost deformed from the starting and stopping and the pressure and tension."

And he concludes, "What they have been able to accomplish has been through hard work."

*TWINS: Coach Jim Matthews
saw the early promise in sons
Jamie and Scott (below, age
four). Right, Jamie as
a player on his dad's
New Washington team*

There is a big difference between athletes and players. The Matthews twins were players.

BEYOND BASKETBALL: Basketball has been a big part of the lives of the Matthews twins, but not so much it obliterated all their other endeavors.

They also played baseball, golf, and tennis. Both became skilled tennis players, with Scott achieving a 70-7 record in high school singles matches.

Both were good students. Jamie ranked second in a class of 70, Scott sixth.

"We have constantly reminded them they will have to earn their livings with their heads, not with their bodies. They are not going to play professional basketball or baseball," Jim Matthews relates. "We insisted they do their homework first, that play came second."

Neither of the twins worked at jobs in the summer, their dad adds. "Oh, they mowed a little grass, but not much. They actually have never done any work, other than school work, or athletic work. They don't even know what chopping tobacco is."

That doesn't disturb Coach Matthews. "When your kids are young let them enjoy their lives, have fun, and grow up. If athletics, or whatever, mean that much to them, give them the opportunity. They are going to work forty to fifty years of their lives anyhow."

THE COACH'S SONS: Jim Matthews tells a visitor he received a lot of criticism over the twins when they were freshmen.

The visitor tells him that isn't unusual.

Matthews laughs: "It was just the opposite here. I was criticized for not playing them enough. We are a small school and even at the freshman level our fans recognized their abilities." Despite calls for them to start, Matthews limited their play the early part of their freshman season.

There were complaints he didn't allow the twins to do all they could do; he also heard objections when he took them out of games to hold down the scores.

There were times when the twins could have scored sixty points, but neither the twins nor Shannon Arthur complained when Coach Matthews removed them from games. "They understood I just didn't believe in embarrassing the other team. I always like to leave the other team with respect."

Jim Matthews heard no criticism about the twins' access to the gym, or to their coach. "I didn't notice any resentment, at least any vicious resentment," says the coach. "That may have been because they had such great success in basketball. Another reason may be because they were always team players. And they made sure that their teammates shared whatever success they have had."

At times, Jim Matthews may have been extra-rough on his sons. "They had to be almost perfect, whereas I may have given a little more slack to the other players. If they threw the ball away, they usually received more criticism than the other players."

The Matthews family tried not to talk about basketball at home. "They would ask how they had played," Coach Matthews says, "and I would tell them they had played well, whether they had or not. I didn't think it was wholesome to be critical at home."

If the twins felt they were under pressure because their father was coach, they didn't show it. But their father admits *he* felt some pressure before the 1989 Madison sectional.

"We had won the sectional the year before and now we were ranked in the state. I wanted our four senior starters to end their high school career on a winning note. If we'd lost the sectional it would have been very negative."

The Mustangs defeated three bigger schools to win their second straight sectional, then ousted New Albany in the regional before losing to Floyd Central, 80-68. It was the end of an era, one New Washington may not soon see again.

AN ANECDOTE: New Washington was having a really close game with Graceland Christian one night when the officials levied a technical against Scott for complaining about a call. "Dad took him out because of that, set him on the bench, and told him to be quiet. A few minutes later Dad got called for a technical, too. He turns to Scott and sends him back in the game. We ended up winning," Jamie relates.

Jim Matthews entered the room when Jamie was telling the story, grinned, and said: "That technical was before I became a calm coach. I'm a lot calmer coach now."

NEW BEGINNINGS: Jamie Matthews was named to the 1989 Indiana All-Star team and played well in the Indiana-Kentucky games. He and Scott were recruited by the University of Alaska at Anchorage, proving correct their father's assessment they deserved a shot at Division I competition.

Both are considering coaching careers. And both say, if they do become coaches, they will model themselves after their dad. "He had a winning attitude, he was a competitor. He was a winner."

Someday they would like to coach their sons, just like their dad coached them.

Jim and Sugie Matthews stayed in New Washington, the house quieter with their sons gone. Jim hoped to rebuild the Mustangs around senior Shannon Arthur and continue to win. Mrs. Matthews continued to be principal at Riverside School in nearby Jeffersonville.

A Boy Full of Surprises

COACH MIKE SORRELL AND SON RYAN

A lot of coaches have expectations of hardwood stardom for their sons.

That wasn't the case for Mike Sorrell. His oldest son, Deron, didn't play. And he wasn't sure his son Ryan had any aspirations to play varsity basketball until he was in high school.

"I had always thought Ryan had more physical ability as a football or baseball player," he explains. "He played varsity baseball and could have been an outstanding football player. Since I thought his natural talents leaned in those directions, I didn't encourage him a lot toward basketball."

Even Mike Sorrell, father, coach, and experienced judge of basketball talent, was surprised when Ryan developed into a solid player, who would become good enough to compete at the college level.

Ryan Sorrell may even have surprised himself. As an elementary and junior high student, he admits, "I just wasn't that interested. I didn't have the desire to play extra. I just went to practices and played games, but I didn't want to work at it. I didn't think I wanted to devote myself to the game."

That began to change when he was a freshman. By then, his dad had moved from Bedford-North Lawrence to Crawfordsville, where Ryan made the freshman team. It was during that season he decided to dedicate himself to basketball.

After the freshman season, Mike Sorrell used Ryan and three other freshmen in varsity and reserve practices. "To be perfectly honest about it," Coach Sorrell exclaims, "Ryan surprised me. He was heavy and he wasn't fast, but he was deceptively quick, and his defense and ball-handling amazed me. He held his own against older players."

That's when Sorrell, the coach, started taking a closer look at Sorrell, the player. He told his son if he wanted to become a varsity player he needed to lose weight and develop into the best ball-handler on the team because they would need a guard the next season. Even then, Mike Sorrell, insists, "I didn't tell him he had to do those things. I just told him what he needed to do if he wanted to play for me."

Ryan accepted the challenge. He worked each day on fundamentals and drills and ran. He lost twenty to twenty-five pounds over the summer.

The work paid off. By the time practice opened, he was ready for varsity competition. He not only made the team, he started every game.

And nobody was happier than Mike Sorrell when his son developed into a basketball player. Ryan had done what he had to do—on his own.

THE PRESSURES INVOLVED: Mike Sorrell knew there would be some fan resentment against Ryan because he was the coach's son. That was to be expected. Coach Sorrell explains why:

Ryan Sorrell was not a super-flashy kid. And it took some time for fans to appreciate what he was accomplishing for the team. As the point guard, he did much of the ball-handling. That caused a few fans, who didn't know the game, to complain, "That's the coach's son, the ball-hog."

Mike Sorrell said the kids on the team accepted Ryan after only a couple of games. It would be mid-season before the majority of the fans acknowledged that Ryan was a legitimate starter.

But he remained under some pressure from fans throughout the season because he was a sophomore playing ahead of seniors. "People have a difficult time accepting that, especially if the player is the coach's son," Mike Sorrell says.

He adds, "The main problem Ryan had was with people who didn't know him. He wasn't arrogant or cocky. The people who knew him liked him. He was an outstanding student and the faculty liked him. The student body liked him. The people in the community who knew him liked him.

"Yet a few people out in the community who didn't know him would say, 'He's not that good. He is only playing because he is the coach's son.'"

Most of that resentment subsided by the time Ryan became a junior. It was a good year, capped by two superior scoring nights in the 1985 sectional. He had averaged ten or eleven points that season, but netted 28 points in one sectional game and 38 in another to give Crawfordsville the championship.

Those performances again surprised his dad. Scoring wasn't Ryan's forte. "His shot was there that weekend, but scoring wasn't his real strength."

MOVING NORTH: Mike Sorrell had mixed emotions when he was offered the coaching job at Goshen between Ryan's junior and senior seasons. It seemed a good professional move, but it would mean Ryan might have to prove himself again. At the time Ryan didn't want to move.

"We were coming off my junior year and we had some good players coming back. My best friends were players. It was tough to leave all that, to leave the team, to leave my friends, to come to Goshen and to start over my senior year."

The moved worked out for both of them. The transition was easy for Ryan. He was welcomed, his dad says, "with open arms by the community and his teammates." Goshen, at the time, was at "rock bottom," Coach Sorrell adds, winning just nine games in two years. It took some time for the team to jell, but victories started coming in mid-season and the team finished 11-12. It beat two teams in the sectional it had lost to in the regular season, and it lost the 1986 sectional championship game by a single point.

Coach Sorrell credits player Sorrell with helping rebuild the Goshen program. "Without Ryan we could have very well been 0-21. It was not only his leadership on the floor and his playing ability, but he knew what it took to win. His work ethic carried over to other players and that made the adjustment easier."

Ryan grins when he hears what his dad says about the team going 0-21 without him. "I doubt that. They had some really good players here. They just needed some guidance from my dad.'' Whatever! The stage had been set for better things to come. Goshen was 10-11 the following season, then 14-4, and 15-8 in 1988-89.

A LEADER: A player doesn't have to be a coach's son to be a coach on the floor. "Any point guard who is good is like a coach on the floor because he is a maestro out there," Mike Sorrell contends.

Ryan, he adds, was the type who made other players better. "If a player was a good shooter, Ryan would get the ball to him at the right time at the right place. If a player was good at taking the ball to the bucket on the break, he'd get him the ball at the right time. He was very unselfish and he didn't care whether he scored or not. The other kids liked that."

Mike Sorrell calls Ryan "a kid who got the absolute maximum, probably a little more, out of what ability he had."

That may have been because while he was growing up he observed his dad's teams and their practices. He had watched players like Larry Ikerd and Brad Phillips at Bedford. He was around good guards at a key age, even though he had little ambition to play back then.

Mike Sorrell's teams have always emphasized ball control and defense. And that gave Ryan an advantage. "That was the kind of game I am best at. I don't have a lot of athletic ability. I'm just fair. Dad's concept of patience and teamwork allows players with not as much talent to be competitive with teams that have more athletic ability."

PRESSURE: Any child who grows up in a coach's home knows about pressure, Mike Sorrell claims.

"A coach is always under pressure to win. You don't have to tell a kid this is pressure, because he can feel it. He feels it at the dinner table. He knows this may be his dad's job." That, he explains, may be why coaches' sons can deal with pressure on the playing floor better than some other players.

"The last thing I wanted anyone to say was that, 'He's daddy's boy,'" says Mike Sorrell. "I would get on him harder than anyone else. I don't know whether that is particularly fair. But if anyone was going to be mad at him they were going to be mad at him because of him, not because of any favoritism I showed him.

WATCHFUL DAD: Goshen Coach Mike Sorrell was surprised at how his son Ryan developed as a basketball player —after high school, he headed to Taylor University

"I would rather the kids on the team be mad at me for the way I treated him. And that happened. Sometimes in the locker room at halftime I'd get all over him. Then I would see another kid pat him on the back as if to say, 'That's okay.'

"Kids aren't stupid. They could see I wasn't giving him any special favors. So the natural tendency was for them to become protective of him. They could protect him in the community better than I could, they could protect him on the floor better than I could. They could protect him anywhere better than I could."

And he adds, "I knew I loved him. I wanted the kids on the team to love him like they do each other. That's why I made it more difficult for him, so much so they could recognize it. Once they recognized that, he was much more acceptable to them."

Ryan understands: "He did that to make sure everybody on the team and everyone else would know there was no favoritism. He treated me like the other players. Sometimes he was even a little extra harder on me. I'm glad he was like that. It would have been a lot tougher on me if he hadn't been."

When Mike Sorrell talked basketball to his son, he did it at the gym or in his office.

"I never brought up basketball in the car on the way home or at home.

"I wanted him to know when I was talking basketball to him, that I was talking to him as a coach, not as a father. It was a professional relationship. He never talked about what his teammates were doing, if they were staying out too late, or whatever. He wouldn't come to me about those things. He wanted no part of that and I wanted no part of that.

"I wanted him to be my son, but I also wanted him to be a team member. No other player would do that, either. You don't expect that out of other players, so I didn't ask him and he never volunteered."

Ryan Sorrell called his father "Coach" at the gym. "Basketball was basketball and Dad and family were Dad and family," Mike Sorrell adds.

ROLES: It is difficult, Mike Sorrell says, for young men to distinguish at times between father and coach.

"You have to forget you are the boy's father when you are talking to him about basketball. It has to be a coach-player relationship. But if it is not a basketball problem, then it has to be a father-son relationship.

"If we are talking about going to a prom, let's make sure it is a father-and-son relationship and if we are talking about passing or penetrating let's talk as a coach and player. I think it is hard for a son to distinguish between a coach and a father when he is the same person."

AN ANECDOTE: Too many coaches can spoil the player. That's why coaches' sons have an advantage. They have only their fathers as coaches.

Other kids may also have their father, mother, aunt, and uncle.

Mike Sorrell says, "When kids go to their fathers rather than to coaches about basketball questions, that creates problems that it is not conducive to solving."

He turns back to his coaching days at Miamisburg, Ohio, for an example. He had a player there who never took a bad shot in practice. But in games he would go shot-crazy. After two games, Sorrell asked him why he was taking so many wild shots. The player confessed his mother was paying him $1 for every point he scored.

"I told him he wouldn't make a cent if he ended up sitting next to me on the bench. I went to his mother and suggested that she reward him not for scoring, but for assists, shooting percentages or something else that would make him a better player."

She apparently did as Sorrell suggested. Her son averaged 34 points a game, without taking wild shots, and made the All-Ohio team. "That wouldn't have happened if he had continued to have two coaches—his mother and me," Coach Sorrell adds.

BASKETBALL AND LIFE: Ryan Sorrell on basketball: "I think basketball is one of the best teachers of life there is. Almost every concept and every principle you learn in basketball can be applied to your occupation or the way you live your life.

"The ideas of teamwork, loyalty, and cooperation with others, the confidence players instill in each other . . . making each other better . . . all those things help you later in life."

REPEAT PERFORMANCE? Would Mike Sorrell like to coach his youngest son, Brandon?

"I think if the only reason I was still coaching then was to coach my son, it would be the wrong perspective. If you're asking if I'd like to have another Ryan, the answer would be yes. I think it would be very difficult to coach my own son if he wasn't an outstanding player. It would be difficult for him, too. There would be too much pressure on him. I think in that case he might be better off doing something else. But, again, you can't say that arbitrarily. It depends on how important it is for the kid to be on the team. Some kids just want to be a part of the team and to be a part of the program. The game is important to other kids only if they play. They aren't happy sitting on the bench."

Ryan, he adds, would not have been happy as a bench-warmer. "He was too much of a competitor. If he had not been a good basketball player he would have been better off putting his energies toward being a good football or baseball player."

Postscript: Mike Sorrell continued to coach at Goshen. Ryan returned to Taylor University, where his sister Kimberly also is a student, played basketball, and planned to graduate in 1990. Ryan intends to become a doctor and his dad has no doubts he will. "He's such a competitor, I wouldn't count him out of anything. If it means studying twenty-four hours a day, he'll study twenty-four hours a day."

A Special Friendship

COACH DAVE NICHOLSON AND SON DAN

As a basketball player for his dad at Noblesville High School, Dan Nicholson learned lessons that will endure a lifetime.

And Coach Dave Nicholson, too, gained from the experience. It made him even more sensitive to the feelings of parents. He explains, candidly:

"Every parent, if he or she is realistic, watches one individual out on the court. I never get angry at parents who get upset about their sons not playing enough. I don't get offended by that because, no matter how hard you try as a parent, I don't think you can be totally objective.

"Your primary interest is the team and your primary goal is for the team to do well. Still, you have a special interest out there in your son, and, to be honest, you find yourself pulling for that one player."

Yet, Dave Nicholson never gave his son any special favors, not even when he was younger. He was careful not to push Dan in front of other kids, so careful, in fact, he never coached him as a young player. And, he admits, that is one thing he regrets.

"Maybe, I cheated him a little there. We have an excellent Boys Club program and some good people there. But since my profession is coaching, I could have done more to develop him earlier."

But that might have been pushing Dan, and "it might have done more harm than good. I just basically stayed away. I watched him play, but I never got involved in any of his practices or games."

He told his son he didn't have to play basketball. "If you don't want to play, fine. It's not going to be a problem. But, if you do play, you have to do your workouts every day. You have to give the game 100 percent. You are not going to be a part-time player."

Coach Nicholson believed that whatever Dan went into—accounting, business, or whatever he decided to do—he would have to prepare himself.

The same principle would apply to basketball.

Julys and Augusts in Indiana can be unbearably hot, especially on outdoor basketball courts. And Dan Nicholson confesses he didn't have the best work ethic as an underclassman and he wasn't thrilled when his dad would ask whether he had done his workouts.

"Sometimes that would make me mad and I'd storm out to the driveway. I would do my drills, but I wouldn't be thinking about what I was doing. I would be doing them because I was told to."

Coach Nicholson convinced his son of the value of hard work. Dan recalls his dad telling him, "I'm not pushing you to be mean to you as a person or as a player. I'm doing it to push you to your limits and to your goals."

Dan understood that.

During basketball season, father and son agreed, "When we are at the gym, it's basketball, when we are home, we can talk [about basketball], but only if what we say is positive."

Dan said, "When we were on the court, I knew it was business. He was the coach and I was the player. At home, he was my father and I was his son and there was no basketball between us."

HIS BRILLIANT CAREER: Dan Nicholson wasn't very old when some friends of his dad brought a goal for the crib and a label, "Mr. Basketball 198?" A basketball was seldom out of sight after that.

The fact that his dad was a coach may have whetted Dan's interest and made him want to play to please his father. "I think we felt how important basketball was to me," Coach Nicholson explains. That's why he tried to let Dan develop his own interest in the game.

Dan Nicholson was in a class of good guards, some of whom moved or dropped out of basketball along the way. By the time he was in the eighth grade, he had started to make his presence known as a player.

But his dad knew he had a lot of other interests and abilities in areas other than athletics. As an underclassman, he won four or five music awards, and Dave Nicholson told his wife that Dan might be better off staying in the choir. "I'm not sure he will win that many awards in basketball."

Nevertheless, Dan continued to play the game his dad coached. As a sophomore, he was carried on the sectional team and would have been on the regional roster if his name hadn't been Nicholson.

Coach Nicholson had his son and another sophomore on the varsity roster the first week of the tournament, then, to be fair, he let two other sophomores fill those spots for the regional.

Dan was the first guard off the bench as a junior, and his dad realizes now he may have had a "quick hook on him": "He would make one mistake and I would yank him out of the game. If it had been another player I probably would have waited until he made two or three mistakes."

After his junior year, Dan Nicholson wondered whether basketball was worth all the time he was putting into it. "We [he and his dad] sat down and talked about that. I kept working throughout the summer to improve for my senior year. If we hadn't had that talk, I might not have kept playing."

Son Dan became the starting point guard as a senior and his dad says his major contribution was his unselfishness and knowledge of the game.

"Dan didn't have some of the physical abilities other players had, but he knew exactly what we were trying to accomplish, how we should play defense, and how we should attack a defense. He understood the game and made good decisions. I think most coaches' kids do that because they are around the huddles as youngsters and they hear what you say."

Dan Nicholson concentrated on being a good assists man and didn't

"Not only is he my son, he's probably as good a friend as I have." —Coach Dave Nicholson

worry about how often he scored. It helped him to be accepted by his team-mates, who knew he would get them the ball in scoring position.

His dad adds, "Dan always played for the benefit of the team. His main assets were his good decision-making, his ball-handling, and his passing, which led to assists. That made it easier for him to be accepted than it would have if he had been a big scorer."

And Dan Nicholson wanted to win just as much as his dad did. "It is reassuring," Coach Nicholson says, "to know there is at least one player on the team who wants to win as badly as you do."

Dan's concern about other players may be why he turned out to be more of a passer and point guard than a shooting guard. "I felt they might accept me more if I wasn't trying to be an All-American scoring guard," he reasoned.

Dan graduated after the 1987-88 season, and when the next season started it was obvious he would be missed. Some fans let Coach Nicholson know they missed his son. "That gave me a lot of satisfaction," the coach adds.

UNAPPRECIATION DAY: One of the low points for Dave and Dan Nicholson came during a pep session before the 1986 sectional. When Coach Nicholson was introduced, a few students booed. Son Dan whispered to another player, "When I'm introduced, they will boo me, too." The other player said, "Oh! They wouldn't do that."

They did do that! "A large majority of the students did boo me," Dan recalls, adding, "Some kids would have run off and been embarrassed by that. I looked at the player next to me and said, 'I told you so.'

"I figured if the kids who booed me had been good enough, they would be standing beside me. It hurt because the kids felt that way toward my dad and me, but I couldn't let that get to me to the point where I was going to quit."

Coach Nicholson said that incident probably bothered him more than it did Dan. "I had been in coaching more than twenty years when that happened, and I had to think about his emotions and mine, too."

A small minority of fans, some of whom may have been parents of sons cut or dismissed from the team, remained negative when Dan was a junior and senior. But Coach Nicholson explains, "The majority of fans really became very vocal in support of Dan, making sure they drowned out the minority. That was very gratifying. It made me feel better about this school and the community."

Before graduating, Dan Nicholson received the Noblesville faculty scholarship on a secret ballot. His dad calls that "a great compliment" to his son. "It says something about the kind of person he was and is."

NICHOLSON PHILOSOPHY: Coach Nicholson has been coaching twenty-five years, moving from New Ross to Darlington to Benton Central before going to Noblesville. He knows how tough coaching is. At Benton Central his teams won 72 percent of their games, including two sectionals. Yet, he was fired when Benton Central didn't win the sectional the fifth year he was there.

He had told his wife Julia they might be at Noblesville three years, then move on to rebuild another program. It didn't turn out that way. They liked Noblesville, Noblesville liked them, and the 1989-90 season was his fifteenth at the school.

Still, he says, "You almost have to coach like every year is your last year. That allows you to make your own decisions. And if you don't make your own decisions you don't want to be coach anyhow.

"You try to be fair. You make decisions you think are the correct ones and you let the outcome fall where it may."

His coaching decisions have allowed his teams to go unbeaten three seasons (two at Darlington, one at Noblesville) and to win 372 times while losing but 152 games.

Coach Nicholson once told a group of doctors that they would be honored nationally if they were heart surgeons and had a 70-30 success ratio.

IN DAD'S PRESENCE: Dan Nicholson thinks the fact his dad was a teacher as well as a coach helped him become a better student. In junior high, his grades were above average, but not great, "A few A's, a few C's, but mostly B's. When I came into high school, I felt I needed to prove something, so I really hit the books hard. I ended up with a 4.0 my freshman year and studying became a habit."

He finished high school with a 3.8 grade point index. And, he concludes, "Because of the presence of my dad at school, I felt I needed to be the best I could in everything."

A WORD OF ADVICE: Dave Nicholson says whether the father-son, player-coach role works "depends on the personalities of the people involved and their relationships. I have seen so many young kids just brace when their parents try to tell them something. If a coach can give instructions to his son, and if it is received well, I think there would be no problems."

AN ENCORE? If they could replay life, Dan Nicholson says he "definitely would do it over. It made me a stronger person and prepared me for life. If I have a son, I would like to coach him . . . Had I played for someone else, I would have missed a lot of time with my dad. I don't think it would have been as much fun for me."

His father says: "From my point of view as a coach, the positives outweighed the negatives. It was a lot of fun." And, as a result, "We are really close. Not only is he my son, he's probably as good a friend as I have."

Upsides and Downsides

SOME ADVANTAGES OF BEING A COACH'S SON

"I got the keys to the gym anytime I wanted them."
—Jeff Oliphant, who played for his father,
Tom Oliphant, at L&M

* * *

STEVE ALFORD: You get the satisfaction of seeing the results a little quicker. You get to actually experience it with your father. As a coach your father is part of the team so you succeed all the way together, or you fail together. It's great being able to share those kinds of experiences.

MATT WADDELL: Accessibility to the gym is important. As a coach's son I can come over at night and shoot around by myself.

BOBBY ANDREW: I suppose having a ride home from practice every night. On a more serious vein, I suppose I was able to draw on Dad's knowledge more than what the other players were able to. I think that gave me an advantage. He was able to give me that individual attention away from the gym a lot of other kids would like to have been able to have.

I didn't always have access to the gym whenever I wanted it ... but I always knew where the keys were hidden.

MICHAEL ALLEN: One advantage is that coaches can teach their sons the correct methods when they start learning the game. Once you start playing, he can give you attention at home as well as at the gym.

If I don't do something right in the game, he can tell me when I get home. I can think about it and work on it, whereas the other guys have to wait a couple days to get to practice.

BERNIE BUTCHER: I spent a lot of time around the gym. I had more opportunities to be in the gym and to play more and, therefore, learned more about the game than other kids normally would have learned.

MARC SLATON: There are a lot of advantages. I think the biggest advantage is that you always have somebody to support you, no matter what. A lot of kids might miss three or four shots in a row in a game, then go home to parents who ask, "Why did you miss those shots? You had a chance to score eight more points." If your dad is a coach, he knows the game, your mom knows the game. They support you even if you have a bad game.

If it's eight o'clock at night and you want to go shoot basketball, your dad puts his shoes on and goes with you. That's something a lot of kids don't have. They don't have that support.

RIC FORD: You are around the game so much more and that gives you a definite advantage. I knew what my dad wanted every time I went out on the floor.

I'd go scout with him. I became a smarter ball player than somebody whose dad wasn't a coach because I was around the game so much more.

BILLY SHEPHERD: The big advantage I had was that I didn't feel any pressure if I went out and missed my first three or four shots. I didn't have to look over my shoulder at the scorer's bench to see if anyone was waiting to come in for me. I knew I was going to play 30 to 32 minutes every night.

On the other hand, I didn't take advantage of it. I shot a lot but I tried to take a high-percentage shot. That security blanket let me know that if I screwed up I might get yelled at or I might get taken out of the game for a second but I would be put back in and have a chance to prove what I could do.

Accessibility to the gym is a definite advantage. There is nothing like being able to practice where you play. You can shoot outside on a ten-foot goal, but I'll take an hour in a gym to three hours outside anytime. You don't have to worry about the wind or the sun or whether the goal is ten feet on one side and nine feet six inches on the other.

DAVID NULL: The opportunities were there, opportunities not all kids have. Not all kids have a chance to ask their dad for the keys to the gym like I did.

JEFF OLIPHANT: The biggest advantage of playing for your father is that he is always there to make sure you play as well as you can. He also can give you instructions both at home and at school.

That plus the fact I got the keys to the gym anytime I wanted them.

THE ADVANTAGES OF COACHING A SON

"I think the biggest advantage is that you get him up in the morning when you go to the gym. He's going to be in the gym and he's going to work."
—Coach Ron Slaton

* * *

COACH JACK BUTCHER: My sons weren't at every one of our practice sessions when they were younger, but, certainly, if they wanted to come to the gym, or if I wanted to help them work on something, I could bring them to the gym.

I think if you are in the gym and observing things at a very young age it's natural for you to develop an interest in basketball.

COACH JIM MATTHEWS: My twin sons made me look a lot smarter than I really am. Over the years they learned, or they acquired, what it takes to win. Their court awareness, their knowledge of the game, were big advantages. They just didn't make mental mistakes. They could take care of what needed to be done out on the floor without much prompting from me.

COACH GLENN ANDREW: I suppose any parent wants his kids to have the opportunities to play. Maybe coaching lets you give them that opportunity. If you want to play your son at guard, you can play him at guard, if you want to play him at forward you can play him at forward.

As far as my two sons, I think it has made them work harder. I know there were times when Bobby would say, "I wouldn't be out here lifting weights if I knew my dad wasn't out here watching me."

There were some things he did that weren't fun to do, but he did them because I was his dad. If Joe Smith down the road decides not to lift weights, the coach isn't going to know that.

COACH BOB HEADY: I can think of some great father and son combinations and I can't think of too many who have not been successful.

I think a lot of it comes from exposure to basketball. The son of a coach has more time in the gym than most kids and much of that comes at a very young age.

Availability of the gym, going to games, riding on the team bus, sitting on the bench, listening to conversations, are advantages. Sons of coaches know the strategy and game plans that are discussed.

COACH PHIL BUCK: You know where they are every night. You know where they go after practice. One of the problems we have is when we dismiss a young man from practice, and his mother works nights, you don't know where he is. If he lives alone with her, you aren't sure he is getting a warm meal, you are not sure he is eating correctly, you are not sure he is getting enough rest.

I think the biggest advantage is knowing what your kids are doing when they aren't playing for you.

I don't think there is any big advantage. I don't believe that. There is an old-fashioned farm philosophy about me that comes out by just being around a kid. He picks that up or he doesn't. One of those things is that right is right and wrong is wrong. I don't care what law is involved, right is right and wrong is wrong. Forget about the law. I try to relay this to my players. My sons picked that up at an early age.

COACH NORM HELD: I suppose the pride factor is important. You get awfully proud of them if they're able to play in a situation like this [Anderson—a hotbed of basketball].

COACH DAVID LUEKING: You don't have to worry about other people's feelings. You know all the facts related to your son. You know what is going on in his life. I know what my son Mark's grades are. I know about his family. I know what his problems are. I know when he is not feeling well. I have first- hand knowledge and I think that helps.

COACH JOE NULL: I think the real advantage is that it gives us something that we have had in common throughout the years. When I was in high school I liked to hunt and fish and my dad was a part of that.

Much of our relationship [that of Coach Null and his sons David and Sam] has been in our common interest in high school athletics. If we hadn't had that opportunity, I'm not sure how close we would have been.

COACH STEVE DeGROOTE: As coach, I get a front-row seat to watch my sons.

Seriously, a coach can teach his sons every facet of the game. He is more precise with his sons. Maybe we should be that way with other players, too.

A coach's son can go to the gym anytime and work out. Others don't have that opportunity.

Coaches' kids know the game better. I remember reading where one college coach said he was able to win a championship because he started five sons whose fathers were coaches.

COACH MIKE SORRELL: I don't believe anyone could have coached my son Ryan any better than I did. We took advantage of his full ability, we put the ball in his hands. and he was able to get 100-110 assists a year. We ran an offense that was conducive to his style of play. We placed him in a college that was conducive to his style of play and his ability.

I provided him an opportunity as a coach he couldn't have been pro-vided—or might not have been provided—by just anybody. It was a good deal for him in some ways, too. But there is no doubt that I got a lot more out of it than he did.

COACH RON SLATON: I think the biggest advantage is that you get him up in the morning when you go to the gym. He's going to be in the gym and he's going to work.

Another advantage is that there is not someone feeding him misinforma-tion [as other players might get from their parents]. There is none of this, "You have to score 27 points because someone else has." In our case, it's, "You can score 27 points if that's what you need to do to help us." When you give him the information as a coach you can tell him what you want and he's not going to go home and get some different information from Mom and

Dad. There's a possibility I may not give him the right information as a coach, but he is not being fed two different things.

COACH AL TUCKER: If I opened up the gym, Brad and Chad were there. When they were older, I'd send them over and they would open the gym up for me.

They were usually in the gym or at home or at the homes of friends playing on outside courts.

An advantage is the fact you expose them not only to your basketball knowledge, but basketball in general. They followed other teams in the area and went with me to scout games. So, by the process of osmosis, your kids are subjected to this. If you are fortunate, they develop an interest in it.

COACH JIM HAMMEL: I was fortunate I could be with my kids a lot during a very important part of their lives. I think coaches are with their sons more than most parents.

You know, in basketball, we start October 15 and hopefully play until March 31. We're just together literally hundreds of hours. When you have that opportunity to be with your own kids, it's something you cannot buy.

PLAYERS ON THE DISADVANTAGES
OF PLAYING FOR THEIR DADS

"You always have to be home before the team curfew. It doesn't take a phone call to catch you."
—Billy Shepherd, who played for his dad, Bill, at Carmel

* * *

STEVE ALFORD: If you have a bad practice or a bad game, you have to go home with the coach. And that's never a lot of fun.

SCOTT HEADY: You don't get to do a lot of other things. Basketball was my whole life when I was growing up. I played three to four hours a day every day every summer.

You have to give up a lot, your weekends, your nights—while other kids are out going to movies and doing other things. You get a chance to do those things once in a while, but maybe not often enough.

That applies, even now that I'm a coach and not a player. I'm here in the gym in the summer six to seven hours a day and a lot of that time I'm not getting paid.

BILLY SHEPHERD: You can't get home late. If you have a twelve o'clock curfew you have to be in at twelve o'clock. There is no way to get in at 12:15. It doesn't take a phone call to catch you.

Seriously, though, the only disadvantages for me came early when I was trying to prove myself. Once I did, it became much easier.

JOE BUCK: You have an awful lot of pressure. The student body may think your father is treating you with favoritism, whether it is true or not. Some people will say the only reason you are playing is because you are the coach's son. You not only go through that, but your family members go through that. They hear a lot of mean comments in the stands and a lot of mean things at the uptown cafe.

But if a kid is strong there are more advantages than disadvantages. If a kid succumbs to the pressures, it can be very harmful.

SCOTT AND JAMIE MATTHEWS: It is hard for a coach to play his son who is a freshman ahead of other kids who are seniors. It's doubly difficult when he has twins who are freshmen, even though they are better players than the other kids. You catch a lot of heat that way.

BOBBY ANDREW: You obviously have to take criticism. At the time, I didn't think it was fair. I had to deal with a lot of other things that other players didn't have to deal with. They could come ready to play basketball and that's all they had to think about. I had to wonder whether Dad would get chewed out by so-and-so or whether I would get screamed at.

Maybe it was a disadvantage because I wasn't able to let it out. Other players could go home and say, "Well, Coach really screwed up tonight." I was never able to do that.

BRETT ANDREW: The biggest disadvantage is hearing kids calling you names like "Daddy's boy." But that just makes you want to play harder. I didn't think I would make the varsity as a freshman, but I did. All that gave me the incentive to keep right on working at it. As the coach's son, I have to work harder. He expects more out of me.

RIC FORD: You know there are people out there who will be against you no matter what you do. That applies, though, even if you are not the coach's son. There will be a few people out there who think you shouldn't be playing.

MARC SLATON: Probably it's the jealousy and crap you have to put up with. People say the reason you are playing is because you are the coach's son. If you are the coach's son, you have to live with the fact that some people will think you are not good enough to play. That happens regardless of how good you may be.

DAVID NULL: As the coach's son, you might become a little more tentative, especially in your shot selection. Of course you never want to take a bad shot. But sometimes you might pass up a good shot because you think your dad might take you out of the game if you miss. You are just afraid to make mistakes.

COACHES—ON THE DISADVANTAGES
OF COACHING THEIR SONS

"A son cannot escape the coach. He has to play for the coach, go home with the coach, live with the coach. He doesn't have the opportunity to just be a boy."
—*Dave Lueking, Austin, who coaches his son, Mark*

* * *

COACH SAM ALFORD: You are always living in the public eye. It makes it tough from the standpoint that people think a coach's son is supposed to be good. That's not necessarily true. A coach's son does have some advantages, but that doesn't necessarily make him a great basketball player and I think the public sometimes expects him to be.

I was very hard on my two sons. I was very hard on Steve. I was hard on Sean, but I did back off a little on Sean from what I learned with Steve. I put a lot of burden on Steve's shoulders. I made him responsible for getting the team fired up, he was responsible for keeping the team in line, he was responsible for making sure everyone was ready to play. I expected him to do an awful lot of things and I know that when you are seventeen there is a lot of life you'd like to live without having to do all those things.

COACH JIM MATTHEWS: The hardest thing for me was the recruiting process, trying to evaluate the ability of my twin sons as to what level they could play in college.

Being a father and being a coach and being very familiar with them, I felt they could play Division 1. When I talked to college coaches, they said they are too small. Usually my answer was, "Would you recruit Jay Burson?" They'd say, "Sure, we would." My next question was, "Did you recruit Jay Burson when he was in high school?" And they said, "No."

(The Matthews twins were recruited by Alaska/Anchorage, a Division 1 school.)

COACH BOB HEADY: If the son of a coach lacks a little ability, you have to make a decision. You have to decide whether you are putting him ahead of someone else because he is your son.

If you have a son who is playing and the team has a terrible season and the coach is getting a lot of heat, the kid hears it. And he knows they are talking about his dad. Luckily that didn't happen to Scott and I. We were lucky enough to have success.

COACH PHIL BUCK: The biggest disadvantage is the pressure the son puts on himself. He wants to be successful in his dad's eyes. If he isn't a star or he isn't scoring a bunch of points and the team gets beat, I think the son feels like he is responsible for Dad's failure. I think that is awfully hard for a young man to handle.

COACH DAVID LUEKING: A son cannot escape the coach. He has to play for the coach, go home with the coach, live with the coach. He doesn't have the opportunity to just be a boy. We all do silly things, make mistakes. Maybe as a father and a coach I don't tolerate that from him. I expect him to be a model individual. In reality, it is better that he makes a mistake now and then just so he can be normal. Instead, he has to perform and be perfect at all times.

COACH BILL SHEPHERD: I don't know that there were too many disadvantages in our case. We were fortunate enough to be very successful. I don't think there were too many negative things that developed from it.

My sons never complained in later years that I tried to make them do too much, or that they were unhappy with what I tried to do, or that I tried to force too much on them.

I don't think that was ever the case. And I think it could be, especially if a son doesn't have that deep desire to excel.

Sometimes a coach might want success for his son and for himself as a father and as a coach, but the kid doesn't want it as bad as his dad wants him to have it.

COACH STEVE DeGROOTE: You are tougher on your own sons. The first year Cory played for me he missed some shots and I got on him. My assistant coach, reminded me, "If that hadn't been your son, would you have been as upset?" I knew I wouldn't have been. He was a good shooter. The shots just didn't go in.

I think a coach has a tendency to put too much pressure on his son. You are too critical at times. You want him to be greater than the others.

COACH DAN BUSH: I think it might be tougher on Alan [my son] than me. I'm not really concerned about what people think about me. I want to be fair with him.

Sometimes people are cruel. Sports brings out the best in people. It also brings out the worst. There will be somebody who doesn't have any idea how many hours we put in in the weight room or in the gym, or how many miles he runs. That person will say the only reason he is playing is because his dad is coach. Anybody who knows me knows I like to win too much. If he's not going to help us win, he won't be out there. But if I think he will help us, he will be there.

If he can come out here, score 20 points a game, get 10 rebounds and never turn the ball over, somebody will say the reason he is playing is because he's my son.

COACH RON SLATON: The jealousies you have to fight. In the four years we were here [at Wabash], there were times when my son Marc passed the ball when I'd just as soon he had not. I knew the player he passed to wasn't going to make the shot. But he did what was automatic, using the instincts that he had been taught.

Other people were jealous of him because he scored a lot of points. He did score a lot because he could shoot. So you fight that jealousy, that dissension. That just kills you. And there is no way to offset it.

COACH JOE HART: You and your son are always in the public eye.

Fans will say, "He [the coach] is letting him do this or he's going to leave him in after he misses five shots because he is his son."

You are always going to have that. You are going to have it if he hits six shots in a row.

COACH JIM HAMMEL: I think the fact that they [sons of coaches] can't lead a normal high school life. They always have to be on guard. Any step out of line will be magnified. That's a lot of pressure to put on a kid.

I've coached twenty-one years of varsity basketball. I've been out there long enough to know that that's just going to happen. But for them [my sons], it's new and I sometimes think it's hard to take.

An Afterword:
Beyond Basketball

All fathers and mothers, are, in their own way, coaches. They prepare their sons and daughters for a bigger game than basketball; they direct them for the long walk down life's winding road.

Basketball, like other sports, mirrors life. Some days it's a victory, other days it's a defeat. But always there is another game, another day.

The coaches in this book acknowledge there is more to life than basketball. But they know, too, that the competition, the discipline, the camaraderie will remain with their sons after the final gun has sounded.

Coach Dave Nicholson summarized it well:

"Sons who have played for their fathers have a mental toughness other kids may not have. And it will help them later regardless of whatever walk of life they take."

And, for any parent, he adds:

"If my son Dan had not played basketball, that would not have made any difference to me. What is important is what kind of kid he, or any teenager, will be five to six years down the road. The main thing is for kids to be taught to make good decisions in life. That's what is important."